CW01664684

ENTREPRENEUR SECRETS

COACHES, CONSULTANTS & EXPERTS SHARE THE SECRETS TO THEIR SUCCESS

AFSHEEN SHAH ANGIE ATES-CLARK
ANNE VRYONIDES HEATHER STEWART
DR JULIETTE HOBSON KATIE FARRELL KELLY TAN
KIMBERLY J BENOIT KRYSTAL CHAMPLIN-GERAGE
MEGAN DOUGHERTY YURY LEVCHENKOV

INSPIRED WORLD PUBLISHING

CONTENTS

INTRODUCTION

Entrepreneurship: the activity of setting up a business or businesses, taking on financial risks in the hope of profit

There's a widely shared meme on the topic of entrepreneurship that I've seen doing the rounds on social media that shows 'a day in the life of an entrepreneur' with a line that juts up and down representing the highs and lows most entrepreneurs face on a daily basis:

"I'm excited"

"Ugh, this is hard"

"It's working!"

"I messed up"

"Give up the good for the great!"

"I think I'm going bankrupt!"

"I"m good. I don't know why I get so down on myself"

"I was wrong. I suck!"

"Wait a second. My life is great"

As someone who has spent the past ten years running a business, first as a side hustle, and for the past 7 years as a full-time entrepreneur, this totally resonates with me!

Being an entrepreneur is not for the faint of heart. You will experience the highest of highs, and often these will be preceded by the lowest of lows.

I've had my fair share of Dark Night Of The Soul moments over the years. Moments where I've found myself crying tears of frustration, asking myself why things haven't worked out how I'd planned.

But there have been, and continues to be, so many highs and amazing moments of pride and happiness. Seeing my clients become published authors or watching them get featured in the press and witnessing them sharing their message in a bigger way, so that they create a much bigger impact in the world, still brings me so much joy and reminds me why I do what I do.

In *"Entrepreneur Secrets: Coaches, Consultants & Experts Share The Secrets To Their Success"*, 11 inspiring entrepreneurs from across the globe share the behind-the-scenes of their success.

The contributors have shared their personal journeys of how they overcame the challenges and obstacles that have led them to where they are now, and how they followed their dreams to create the businesses they have today. They also share their tips, advice and expertise on how readers can have more success in their own life and business.

Their personal accounts include everything from dealing with divorce, illness and emotional breakdowns, to overcoming stress and burnout, career reinvention, spiritual awakening and more.

Their stories are touching, inspiring and motivating and their practical tips and advice will genuinely help you to elevate your life and business.

Enjoy their stories, learn from their wisdom and like these authors have done, follow your dreams. As Steve Jobs said: "Your time is limited, so don't waste it living someone else's life. Don't be trapped by dogma – which is living with the results of other people's thinking. Don't let the noise of other's opinions drown out your own inner voice. And most important, have the courage to follow your heart and intuition. They somehow already know what you truly want to become. Everything else is secondary."

Dina Behrman
PR Strategist and Publisher at Inspired World Publishing
Find out more at www.dinabehrman.com

1

AFSHEEN SHAH

PLANTING FLOWERS IN THE DESERT

I had just turned 43 and was recently single after walking away from a five -year relationship I had thought I would spend the rest of my life in. I'd also just been told that pregnancy was no longer a viable option following a botched surgery. I felt as if my life and my body had betrayed me. And just like that, nearly every dream I had held for so long had been shattered within a year.

To add insult to injury, the auto-immune issues I had spent over a decade so carefully managing and controlling spiralled back out of control only a few months later. Boyfriend ...gone...babies I'll never know as mine or get to hold... and my well-being ...going downhill, I kept asking the same two questions "*why is this happening to me?* and "*where did I go wrong*?" I felt depleted, depressed, and incredibly alone. All of this even compromised my ability to work. For a second time, I felt as if life itself, and my body, had betrayed me yet again.

My world felt desolate. I had always thought of myself as a survivor —a fighter even —but after that year, I couldn't help but question if I had any fight left to give. Even the joy of doing the things I loved seemed to have disappeared.

And then came the judgment. I'm not sure what felt worse: the judgment from others or my judgment of myself. Between working in an industry that based a person's worth on their ability to achieve and perform and being raised in a culture that often based a woman's worth on her status as a wife and mother, I soon felt like an outcast and complete failure. I started to question my own worth as a woman, my purpose, and sometimes even my desire to live. Unmarried and childless, I no longer felt like a real woman.

My confidence and self-worth started to decline. What I didn't realize then was that the more I lost faith in myself, the more others lost theirs in me also.

So I worked even harder and longer hoping to regain confidence in myself and the approval of those around me. I mistakenly believed that if I could just do and be more than I already was, the world would finally see my value. And if the world could see it, maybe I would too. I spent the next two years saying *yes* to almost everything I should have said no to and *no* to everything my body, mind, and soul was screaming at me to say *yes* to. Work dinners, networking events, weekend workshops and charity drives completely filled my schedule while rest, self-care, and most of all, the self-love I needed continued to be ignored. And in the little free time I had left each week, I made sure I somehow made it to every birthday, wedding, wedding shower, baby shower, christening and holiday party that I was invited to. I fueled my days with caffeine and Adderall and numbed my nights with whisky neat. I said yes to everyone and everything but myself. I said *yes* to everyone and everything but myself.

Whenever a doctor would tell me to dial back my work hours, I would take on more projects and work longer hours instead. When they told me I needed to switch to lighter activities at the gym to reduce the inflammation that was wreaking havoc on my body and my brain, I defied them by signing up for more marathons and obstacle courses. Anything to prove to others (and myself) that I mattered.

Throughout it all, I ignored my intuition and own needs. And in doing so, I turned my back on the two things I needed most to truly keep going: my health and sanity. I knew I was burning myself out, but I couldn't bring myself to stop. It wasn't long before my personal and professional lives were negatively affected. I sensed that I was headed for disaster, but the uncertainty of having no path at all seemed worse than continuing down this path I was on.

My life felt like a minefield of unfulfilled dreams and hopes. It didn't matter which way I turned, things seemed to be blowing up, blowing away, or simply blowing past me as I tried desperately to make it all stop and frantically grasp onto the shards of the only reality I knew. With my health continuing to decline, my love life in shambles, and the career I had worked so hard to build slipping through my fingers, I felt too paralyzed with fear to take a step in any direction —in case it turned out to be a misstep.

REACHING BREAKING POINT

The breaking point came after an adoption I had already spent three years waiting for was unexpectedly put on indefinite hold with no guarantee that it would move forward. And the adoption company I had been working with suddenly had no answers to any of my questions. I made the painful decision to walk away from the company, only to discover that I was now "aged out" of most adoption programs and needed to be married to adopt from most others. With no one to truly turn to or talk to, I found myself experiencing what would become the second dark night of my soul.

Not long after, I found myself lying in my bed, in complete darkness and solitude, unable to find the mental or physical strength to get up or get going. I was physically, emotionally, and mentally depleted. I had nothing left to offer to anyone, not even myself.

All the joy, love and zest I had once felt for my life had disappeared entirely. And I had no idea how to get it back. How could I when I had done everything I was supposed to and told to do and it still didn't work out?

I found myself angry at the world, at God, and most of all, at myself. This wasn't how it was supposed to turn out. I had done everything, checked all the boxes and followed the straight and narrow path. And yet here I was, sad, stagnant, and stuck while everyone else seemed to be moving on with their lives and turning dreams into reality. I let my tears stream down for hours that day, curled up, as my gentle giant of a dog sat next to me, patiently licking them off my cheeks until they finally stopped flowing. I cursed God. I cursed the Universe. I cursed anything and everything that crossed my mind. And in the process, years of pain, tears, and unfelt emotions were finally set free from my body. Each loss I had failed to acknowledge and every emotion I had buried alongside it surfaced that night, begging for my attention, which I willingly gave to them. It was only when I finally embraced the pain that it started to set me free.

When I woke up the next day, I knew something had shifted. I also knew it was time to take matters back into my own hands. I started with my health and then moved into every other area of my life.

ONWARDS AND UPWARDS

I got rid of foods, habits, thought patterns and even people that were clearly toxic for my body and my soul and replaced them with things that made my soul feel alive. I read almost every book I could find on creating inner peace and allowed Gabby Bernstein, Jack Canfield and Wayne Dyer to become my virtual mentors. Daily meditation became my therapy. And my dog's unconditional love became my reason for getting up and finding joy in each day. The more I removed the things weighing me down, the more I made room for things to propel me upward —and forward.

I also took a good hard look at myself and the role I had played in getting to where I was. Facing yourself can be the most challenging thing when you don't like where you are or who you've become. And what I saw wasn't all that pretty at first. In truth, everything that had led me to that point had been somehow the result of past decisions. I had been so stuck in my own sadness and self-pity that I had stopped living up to my potential and showing up for myself in the way I deserved.

Motivated by the changes I had already started seeing, I chose to start making better decisions for myself, ones that would help me heal and find a way to love life and myself again. And most of all, I stopped looking to others for what was already inside of me.

I also stopped looking at life as something I was passively enduring and started looking at it as something I could instead be actively creating.

This process revealed to me just how important mindset is in creating the life we want. In order to create a life I truly loved, I had to learn to make choices that promoted that life. I had to choose *myself*. Being a naturally caring person and having been raised to be a people pleaser, learning to put my own needs first was probably one of the biggest shifts I had to make. Being a naturally caring person and having been raised

Inner work and mindset training soon became the cornerstone of my morning routine. The more I strengthened my mind, the more resilient my body and my spirit became. And when I realized how powerfully I could process and move emotions out of my body due to the inner work, I knew I had to share this gift with others. This led to my first certification as a mindset coach and transformational trainer.

Using the tools I had learned in my training, I completely shifted the thoughts and beliefs I had created about myself, my worth and even my chronic illness. I finally stopped looking to others for approval and validation.

Throughout the process, I kept following the breadcrumbs, doing more of what was working and reducing (in some cases, eliminating entirely) those things that were no longer working for me.

Having my dreams fall apart was one of the biggest gifts life could have handed me. Falling apart forced me to face parts of. myself that were no longer serving me and release them so I could put myself back together in a way that was better aligned with who I wanted to be, not who society or others thought I needed to be. It also helped me realize that I had spent most of my life living and chasing dreams others had created for me.

FINDING THE JOY

Soon, the areas of my life that were previously lonely and desolate became filled with joy and beauty. And like the lone flower that finds its roots in the middle of a barren desert, I found myself standing tall and strong in my aloneness.

Once we accept and embrace our role and responsibility in creating our own outcomes, we can create a more fulfilling and meaningful life. There's undeniable freedom in learning to love- and be grateful for- every part of your life. Even the not-so-pretty ones and those parts those you wouldn't willingly want to repeat. We all have parts we haven't faced or would rather not see. Instead of shunning them, open the door to them and invite them in. That's how they lose their hold over you, and that's how you set yourself free. Most people think of emotion as a weakness. However, shutting the emotion out is easy; the real work begins when we actually face them and learn how to work through them and *with them*.

That's where the mindset work became so important for me in healing my illness and my heart. I no longer allow external factors (including my relationship status!) or achievements to determine my worth. My worth is now a factor in how I show up for myself and, more importantly, in how I see myself. Unsurprisingly, the more I became my own compass for determining my worth, the better I started to feel—mentally, emotionally *and physically*. I still love my morning cup of coffee, but now I have it because I can. I also still enjoy a good cocktail on the weekends, but I no longer need to numb myself with one every night since the pain I was so busy avoiding has instead become the basis of my power.

Mindset work is about so much more than reframing how we see things. It's about harnessing the power of our mind to create a deeper connection between our mind, body, and spirit. Our mindset shapes our beliefs and influences how we think, behave and respond in different situations. And when that response comes from a place of alignment within our mind, body, and spirit, we act from a place of true, internal power. And if we can learn to tap into that inner power, there is virtually nothing that isn't possible or available to us.

CHANGE YOUR THOUGHTS TO CHANGE YOUR LIFE

The mindset work I did on my personal journey allowed me to create true alignment within myself and my needs, which led me down the path of coaching others to do the same. Mindset work forms the foundation of my coaching programs. I genuinely believe that if we can learn to change our thoughts, we can change our entire experience of life, regardless of the events that may be unfolding around us.

Many of us have learned to see our minds as an enemy and something that holds us back. And with phrases like "you're your own harshest critic" and "it's all mental" or "mind over matter" being thrown around all the time, it's easy to see why people start to see their minds that way as opposed to a tool that they can use to create transformation. I help my clients change their relationship with their minds in a supportive and empowering way and look at parts of themselves that they may have been too afraid to look at before.

We all have parts we haven't faced and would rather not see or expose to others. Instead of shutting the door on them, invite them in. That's how they lose their hold over you, and that's how you set yourself free.

I believe everyone deserves to live a deeply fulfilling and meaningful life on both a personal and professional level. Through mindset work, I help my clients cultivate the mental, emotional and physical resilience needed to successfully navigate difficult decisions and challenging situations so they can create their own oasis full of blossoming flowers.

I believe every part of our journey, no matter how painful, offers us a gift, a lesson or opportunity for transformation. True success in life comes once we learn to welcome and embrace each of those options.

So wherever. you are in your own journey, look for the gift, the lesson or transformation possible for you. It's in there somewhere. You just have to be willing to take a stand for it and say YES to yourself.

ABOUT THE AUTHOR

AFSHEEN SHAH

Afsheen Shah is a mindset and empowerment coach who works with high achieving women who are struggling to find balance and deeper meaning in their life. She helps them to uncover and reframe patterns and beliefs that may be keeping them stuck so they can find lasting fulfillment in their personal and professional lives. Afsheen received her certification through the prestigious Elementum Institute and is committed to changing women's lives all across the world so they can live life unapologetically and on their own terms, free of societal restrictions and judgments. In addition to her own blog, Afsheen has contributed thought provoking pieces to the Tiny Buddha and Mind Life Spirit publications. Afsheen lives in New York with her two rescue dogs who she says are a constant reminder for her to always stop and smell the flowers and live life with joy in your heart and a spring in your step.

Website: www.afsheenshah.com
Instagram: @afsheen shah

2

ANGIE ATES-CLARK

THE SECRET SAUCE OF SUCCESSFUL ENTREPRENEURSHIP

Entrepreneurship consists of Purpose, Passion, Protocols and Profit—if you have the 'secret' sauce of clarity to make it happen.

I jumped onto the entrepreneurial train after 20 years in corporate America. My spouse was less than supportive at the time due to the fact I was 'brain trained' in corporate culture. He did not think I had 'it' or the acumen in me to be an entrepreneur like he was. After all, I only knew the corporate structure and bosses who guided me in what to do. An entrepreneur *is* the boss. Despite my spouse's thinking that my new business was really a 'hobby', I went on to create multiple six-figure clinics.

What I quickly realized was that all my standard operating procedures (SOP), KPIs, and conscious communication training would play a huge role in my business success.

I will share a few stories of challenges and setbacks; however, the most important for me is to share with you the implementable takeaways that, if followed, will ensure your *purpose* is fueled by your *passion* and ultimately your *protocols* cultivate *profit*! Oh, and learn the 'secret sauce'!

I will primarily be focusing on my experience as a natural health practitioner. My viewpoint will be working in integrative health care with clients. You may call yourself a health coach, naturopath, holistic consultant or whatever the title, but in the end, you work with clients, guiding them on a holistic journey to health.

There are many reasons an entrepreneur becomes a business owner. First, there is a calling, a purpose from inside driving you to take this step. Secondly, you may be sick and tired of being controlled by corporate or boss directives and want to be your own boss. Whatever the reason, WELCOME to being a business owner!

You get that perfect idea and dream of its success. You create a business plan and it all looks great on paper. Or maybe you just jump, knowing that this is what you want and will make it work. The key is having the 'secret sauce' of *clarity* as you begin the journey of owning your business. Knowing where you are going from location, business contents, client attraction methods and more. Clarity is the 'secret sauce' that will ultimately determine your profits!

"It's a lack of clarity that creates chaos and frustration. Those emotions are poison to any living goal." - Steve Maraboli

---

As you get all excited about this new adventure and opportunity, the naysayers will come out of the walls, from under the couch, and even from those you respect.

You know, the ones who project their fear upon you. They mean well, for the most part, but they just can't envision you doing it on your own. Many times they could not or would not take this very exhilarating yet intimidating leadership step. Therefore, they are there to ensure you don't fall or get hurt. Since they couldn't stand in their genius, they simply cannot fathom you standing in your genius! This will be your first challenge as an entrepreneur. Remaining strong with the passion inside, knowing that this is what you are called to do is essential to the 'secret sauce' of clarity.

Joining the ranks of business ownership and becoming a traditional naturopath practitioner was a path I was pushed down. I left corporate America due to debilitating autoimmune diseases. This began my journey into natural health. I ultimately took certifications after certifications, and it seemed so natural and invigorating to learn all the 'stuff'. I organically moved into helping others and sharing what I was learning. I then decided it was time to 'do this thing' and began seeing clients for money. I no longer was doing this as a side hustle hobby but now as a professional career.

I was a professional Board Certified Naturopath creating results-driven wellness plans.

TAKEAWAY #1- BOUNDARIES

You must establish boundaries from the beginning. Boundaries of how, when, and where your clients will interact with you. An actual 'protocol' or system for client onboarding, wellness plan contents and follow-up. Boundaries with family and friends, because this is your business now. When they go into their work/job, they expect to be compensated and so do you. This phase is all about posturing up and building your confidence while letting your passion guide the path.

I initially would see clients anytime—literally any time of day and any day of the week. WHY? Because I was so determined to make this thing work. All the naysayers frequently reminded me how this was a fun hobby, failing to acknowledge that I was a professionally trained practitioner offering services. I quickly realized I could not keep this pace up and still maintain my role as a spouse and mother. There was a lot of growth during my first few years.

I came from my identity being tied to a corporate title with achievements to my own boss where no one cared about my titles; they wanted results. Partner that with the self-worth and confidence challenges because I was equating both with the respect and belief that I was not getting from those I thought would support me.

This is why I am so adamant about you getting CLEAR on just what this role of entrepreneurship looks like. What hours do you want to work? What days, etc. STICK TO IT! I learned that my clients would create time to work with me if they felt they would get results. *This is how you avoid burnout!* Have FAITH and stand strong.

Action steps:

Using your 'secret sauce' of clarity - determine what boundaries are needed.

Family boundaries - Do you have dedicated time just for them? If you work from your home office, do you have dedicated time so that you are not interrupted?

Client boundaries - What does an ideal work week look like? How do your clients contact you? How often can they contact you? During what hours?

Your purpose and vision (clarity) are at the center of your life and they radiate out and are expressed in all areas of your life. This determines your internal boundaries.

I grew from working with clients in the back room of health food stores and a chiropractor's office to renting my own space. This is when the SOP knowledge really kicked in. I began following principles from Michael Gerber's book *The E-myth* and putting my clinical twist on it. I began structuring and creating protocols for all actions and processes in my office. This afforded me the opportunity to employ part-time assistance because the new hire training was self-contained. There were reference documents (protocol), for ordering products, paying bills, answering phone calls and more.

This also allowed me to make a decision once, document it, and then have it for reference when I simply did not recall what we had done before in this situation; because this will happen. When I systemized my office and client care processes I began increasing my productivity and profit.

I then leveraged my time and client results with these structured and systemized protocols. I created programs and packages for my clients. This increased the lifetime value of my clients and increased my profit.

By delivering beyond expectations, from onboarding through follow-up, my referrals increased. Naturally, I then cultivated a formal referral program protocol, again determining the lifetime value of my clients and then rewarding referral bonuses based on that number.

TAKEAWAY #2- STRUCTURE, SYSTEMS, STREAMLINING

You will never be able to 'scale' if you have not created systems and protocols within your business. Develop these early because your business's value is based partly on *can 'anyone' operate it successfully.*

Determine what steps you repeatedly do and then automate them. Maybe it is recording some client education on a topic or topics that you always spend time in your session speaking about and then providing that to them on their time, not yours.

An example: Let's say you always speak on the topic of water. Instead of fumbling for a handout, a book or a YouTube video on the topic, record a quick video with the information they need to know. If you are not video-familiar, then create a document that is easily accessible for you to include in their wellness plan. This will save you hours of time and resources.

Create protocols that allow you to document and forget it. As you expand and scale, you will not be able to recall what you did in the same situations last time. You will not be able to control every move or action of your team. Establishing the rules, policies, systems and protocols is the key to leveraged profit.

And if you have no desire to scale, good for you! You can positively impact lives by providing wellness plans on a part-time professional basis. However, the same suggestions apply. There is no reason not to systemize and document processes and protocols for future reference. This will aid you in leveraging your time and delivering life-changing results.

Action steps:

1- Create a list of resources you already have that can be converted or shared with your clients. Organize those resources so you (or your team) can easily access and share them.

2- Commit to ONE protocol created that positively impacts your bottom line profit. Take action this month on this one protocol.

"Organize around business functions, not people. Build systems within each business function. Let systems run the business and people run the systems. People come and go but the systems remain constant" (Michael Gerber, E-Myth Revisited).

Now it was time to truly begin building my business outside of my referral program.

You can choose many ways to build your business; however, you can not do them all effectively. Whatever you choose to do, the key question is *clarity*—"what do I want the outcome to be?"

TAKEAWAY #3- SECRET SAUCE – CLARITY IN BUILDING MY BUSINESS

Some people will choose to use social media platforms to build their businesses. There are numerous opportunities and various ways to use social media. However, my caution is that if you are a solopreneur, the reality of being able to manage multiple social media platforms is exhausting. Find out where your core clients hang out and consistently work within that platform.

When consulting with practitioners, I find they think they need a website, multiple social media platforms, Google ads, Facebook ads, lead magnets and funnels from their website, and the list goes on and on. What you need is the 'secret sauce': *clarity*!

Who is your core client? Some people call it your niche; I call it "whom do you love to work with?" Don't worry; there will be others that are referred and join these core clients. However, you will not directly market to those individuals. You will market and work with your core clients. These folks will feed your soul and drive your passion.

I personally love to speak. I find I can connect with my core clients effectively and seriously. I travel all over the world speaking on stages as well as virtual stages. I love to speak to the professionals of the healing arts and guide them on how to shine their genius. There are loads of certifications out there to train the practitioners but none out there to truly train them on a 'beyond coaching' business. I work with medical doctors, other licensed medical professionals, and unlicensed integrative healthcare practitioners guiding them on an aligned path to living their *purpose* fueled by their *passion* and ultimately their *protocols* cultivate *profit*!

The first step to determining just how to cultivate your business success is knowing your client's lifetime value. This affords you the opportunity to have clarity on actions to build your business.

The lifetime value is determined as follows:

1. How long on average will your client use your services? (three months, two years, etc.)

2. How much is the average session/visit fee? (not including supplements)

3. How many on average sessions/visits will the client see you in that length determined in #1?

This equals the lifetime value of your client.

Example: They will see you for 12 months, visiting four times in that timeline with a core session/visit fee of $200 each time. *Lifetime Value is $800.00*

Let me share with you WHY this is so important. If you created a referral program and offered your collaborative partner $100.00 for every client who began your program, wouldn't that be motivating for them? Further, if you were to speak or somehow market your services, you have a baseline of the value of a new client.

Keep in mind that the 'new' client is the most expensive to attain. There are actually three ways to build your business, regardless of what type of business you are in.

1- Attaining new clients - I just determined that this is the most expensive

2- Selling more at one time/visit with the existing client

3- Selling more often to your existing clients

I deep dive into these steps in my Clinical Mastery Mentorship program. Well worth learning these essential aspects of operating a profitable business.

When I started out, I lost thousands of dollars marketing to the wrong people the wrong way. Oh, I put forth the effort and the hard work. But I learned that even though I was passionate and confident, some folks just simply were not open or ready for my genius to shine. This means time is money! I am not just talking about hard-earned money investments; I am talking about my time and other resources too being invested in the wrong places.

Action steps:

1- Evaluate who you LOVE to work with--your core client. Really step into the imagination of who is in this group. Why do you love working with them? What can you offer them that makes the relationship a win-win? Create that clarity and learn where they hang out and what they need from you.

2- Determine the lifetime value of your client. This will provide you clarity with where to market your services, how to market your services and whom to partner with to market your services.

"As much as you might love running your business, you must have an end-goal in the plan. At the very least, an exit strategy keeps you from turning your business into a glorified job – working from home, but with longer hours."* - *Kevin Donaldson

---

Even though at the beginning of this entrepreneurship decision you have no plans to exit, I encourage you to keep in your mind 'if' you did, are you creating a business that someone else would want?

I am not talking about heading for the door the moment it gets tough; I am talking about celebrating your successes ahead of time. Questions to consider as you cultivate your business are: Will I ever retire? If I do, what happens to all the work I have done? Will I just close the doors? Will I want to sell my client list to someone else? Will I license out my work? And the list goes on.

In my book chapter in the multi-author book *Creating Joy: Changemakers Share Wisdom, Rituals & Practices For Living A Joy-Filled Life*, I speak about completing what '*I was called to do*'. I never planned to sell any of my practices but *God needed me elsewhere.*

God has interesting ways to move you where you are needed on this journey called life.

TAKEAWAY #4- CELEBRATING AN EXIT STRATEGY

I am encouraging you to think about the fact you may not be owning this business forever. This is why I challenge you to look at starting and exiting in one big picture. The more value you can cultivate in your business affords you the opportunity to step outside of it and impact lives when you are needed elsewhere.

What so many professionals of the healing arts experience is job burnout. This is because either they have bought into the lie of 'earn money while you sleep' or they simply refuse to create systems and release the control to the processes while building their businesses.

You have been 'brain trained' to get another certification in a modality or specialist training without any consideration that unless you can implement such training into a financially viable business, you have just secured yourself a bunch of expensive wall hangings. The ultimate exit strategy does not involve how great you are; it involves how great your business is without you.

Being open to other like-minded mentors is the key to developing your exit strategy. And no I am not talking about a business coach who frankly has never walked in your entrepreneurial shoes; I am talking about having a mentor mastermind group with vast knowledge of how to implement all your skills while creating a profitable business and an exit strategy.

Here are four possible exit strategies to consider:

- Sell to Inside Key Employees
- Pass the business on to Family
- Sell to Outside Third Parties
- Planned Liquidation

If you are a solo entrepreneur, you will find burnout the quickest and then comes feelings of isolation. This is when you will be challenged the most to align with your 'secret sauce' of clarity and flow through the 'stuff' and shine your Genius.

I invite you to join our Clinical Mastery Mentorship membership to guide you through the processes of beginning, establishing and sustaining a viable business. The members are just like you! This is not some high-end coaching program with empty promises; this is a mastermind group of healing arts professionals ready to support you in shining your Genius to the world.

"Deliberately seek the company of people who influence you to think and act on building the life you desire." – Napoleon Hill

---

ABOUT THE AUTHOR

ANGIE ATES-CLARK

Angie Ates-Clark is a leading Intuitive Business Strategist who works with female entrepreneurs helping them create a conscious ethos as a feminine leader.

She's spent over 3 decades equipping, empowering and training over 10,000 professionals globally. She's a multiple #1 international bestselling author and recognized speaker.

She spent over 20 years in Corporate Executive Leadership, where she was known for her talent scouting and succession planning strategies.

After multiple autoimmune diagnoses she repurposed her life; educating herself on integrative healthcare solutions including energy medicine. Ultimately launching successful 6-figure health clinics, which served over 5000 clients.

She's been featured in over 250 training videos, multiple summits and served as a co-host of several podcasts.

Whether she's sharing stages with Les Brown or facilitating a Corporate Wellness Program she's regularly 'shaking up the status quo' to inspire people to take action quickly, helping them achieve unprecedented results.

You'll find her traveling the world with her husband Don, or spending time with her 3 children - her inspiration for life.

Email: office@AngieAtes.com
Facebook: www.facebook.com/DrAngieAtes
Website: www.AngieAtesClark.com

3
ANNE VRYONIDES

WHAT IS HOLDING YOU BACK?

"Trauma isn't what happens to you, it's what happens inside of you." - Gabor Mate

---

Tonight was the big night. Everyone decorated their boards and wrote their goals on one side and their obstacles on the other. It was time for the board break, and we divided everyone into small groups. I wanted to participate in the group with our instructor, but my friend wanted to stay in the current group we originally migrated into with some other people she had just met. Reluctantly, I agreed. After the first guy went, I volunteered to go next. I was ready. I had taken so much time to decorate my board. I was proud of my powerful life goals and for acknowledging the obstacles I believe were standing in my way. This was my time, and I was ready to step into my power and overcome what had been holding me back. I stepped up, got into position, and raised my hand up to powerfully lower it down and break the board. However, as I made contact with the board, I realized I had broken the board and my wrist at the same time. My bone was protruding from the side of my wrist, and the pain was excruciating. I was in shock and feeling so much pain. I could observe what was happening around me but couldn't mentally process anything. The event staff quickly took me to the local urgent care, but the nurse told them that they didn't have pain meds strong enough to make me comfortable. Then we proceeded to the ER of the local hospital where I entered alone due to the rigid COVID restrictions. I ended up having emergency surgery that night and left with my right arm in a soft sling. Instead of flying back home across the country to heal my broken wrist, I decided to stay in California and finish my second training week. One evening at dinner, a friend asked if I knew why I broke my wrist during the board break. I said no. She explained that I fractured my wrist because part of me believed I could accomplish my goals and another believed I couldn't overcome my obstacles. WOW! What a painful life lesson in self-doubt.

This newfound awareness drove me to deep-dive into studying the subconscious mind. How could I feel like a confident and powerful woman yet have an underlying current of failure running behind the scenes in my mind? I realized these limiting beliefs that I wasn't aware of were playing out every day of my life. I wasn't consciously aware of what they were, but I knew a negative program was running somewhere in my mind. I always believed I could overcome any obstacle that was presented to me until I was faced with the reality of the physical manifestation of my split mind. I didn't know how to fix this, but I was determined to figure it out and thus began my personal development quest. I was determined to become the best version of myself and to fix all of the limiting beliefs and traumas that were holding me back. I always knew I was destined for greatness, but I didn't know how to get to where I needed to be. I felt so lost. I was working so hard and striving to expand my knowledge, yet I was still searching and longing for the unknown. I didn't know what was holding me back, but I felt like my subconscious mind held the missing piece of my puzzle.

I became obsessed with learning about the subconscious mind and how I could reprogram it to achieve my goals. At the time, I was unaware that my subconscious mind was controlling 95% of my life. That meant that 95% of my brain's activity was unconscious, running on autopilot, and my emotions and behaviors were dependent on this 95% that was beyond my conscious awareness. This revelation explained so much. I began reprogramming my subconscious mind by writing out my daily goals and meditating. I also started studying hypnosis and regression hypnosis to add different modalities to my healing to deeply transform and reprogram my mind. I was also guided to learn about the E4 Trauma Method® and immediately knew it was the missing piece to my healing. This process enabled me to suppress and release the heightened emotions that were trapped around a few traumatic events in my life. After releasing the suppressed emotions, I became aware of the limiting beliefs I had created at the time. This awareness enabled me to release what was no longer serving me and freed me to create new empowering beliefs.

"Who looks outside, dreams; who looks inside, awakes." - Carl Jung

---

So what's holding you back from achieving your dreams? Do you know? Do you feel you're destined for greatness but can't seem to get there? Do you feel like you have taken all of the courses and have the knowledge, but everyone else's road map isn't getting you to the promised land?

What keeps many of us entrepreneurs from reaching our dreams is unresolved challenges from past experiences that impact our behavior and feelings of self-worth, confidence, and commitment.

You may not view it as trauma, but many of us have been through incredibly difficult experiences such as loss, divorce, toxic relationships, tough childhoods, or health challenges. Even if you may not recognize it as trauma, it creates a traumatic response within you and teaches you to behave in a way that doesn't serve you.

If any of these issues resonate with you, you may have experienced a trauma that is still playing out subconsciously in your mind. Trauma may seem unrelated to your success at work, but the brain you use at home is the same one you use for your business. You may be determined to succeed, but your brain may have constructed an unconscious barrier blocking your conscious goals.

If you're struggling with fear, insecurity, or self-doubt that holds you back from pursuing your goals, this could be trauma. Or you could be a perfectionist filled with procrastination. It can seem overwhelming, but these behaviors can be healed.

So what is trauma? Trauma is a period of heightened emotions that transpires during a period of anywhere from 5 minutes to 24 hours when an individual places a negative or positive meaning around an incident that they consider to be highly upsetting. Trauma is commonly thought of as a major physical event like being in a war, a car accident, or physical violence. However, many people experience trauma in the form of relationship breakups, being bullied as children, divorce, narcissistic relationships, or highly upsetting incidents. Trauma is what happens inside of you, the wound you sustain, the meaning you give it, and the way you come to believe certain things about yourself, the world, and other people. It is a disconnection from your authentic self, but it can be restored.

Learning about the effects of trauma and how our mindset impacts our behavior is so important. Realizing that we can choose to create new empowering beliefs and declarations for ourselves instead of allowing our default programming to run rampant in our lives creates an opportunity to heal the painful parts so we can reach for the greatness we all possess.

"When the student is ready, the master appears."
– Tao Te Ching

Unresolved trauma had been playing out in my life for years, and it wasn't until I began my trauma training and working through my own issues that I realized this was what was holding me back from starting my business. I wasted years of my life being stuck and held back by fear and limiting beliefs. Just like a computer program that needs the hard drive cleaned up, reset, and the software updated, we also need to clear out the old programs and viruses that have taken over our minds and that no longer serve us.

Two main traumas were holding me back from my entrepreneurial success. One of my limiting beliefs was from a past life memory. In the flashback scene, I was a slave working on a farm. I could see myself standing next to this horse-drawn carriage and begging the landowner to allow me to take on more responsibility around the plantation, but he refused. I was so angry and upset, and I felt like there was nothing I could do. As I was re-experiencing the regression, I realized during that moment that I had made a decision. I decided that I wasn't enough, that I was a failure, and that I was destined to never live out my dreams. I also decided I was not smart enough; I didn't deserve better; life was not fair, and life doesn't give me the chances it gives others. Wow, this was so impactful. This small snippet of a past life scene held so much trauma, negative emotions, and limiting beliefs. No wonder I could not move forward in my business with all of these limiting beliefs dragging me backward with each step I took. This was the most powerful release I had throughout all of my trauma healing sessions. This exact process helped me clearly see my limiting beliefs so I could finally unlock my entrepreneurial potential. This was part of the epigenetic marks that were imprinted on my DNA at birth. With the unveiling of these new insights, I had the opportunity to create new empowering beliefs for myself. I understood that I get to decide and declare what I want for my life and have the potential and power to do anything I choose. I decided then and there that I would take 100% responsibility for my life, the good and the bad, and that I was worthy of everything I wanted.

The second trauma where I created limiting beliefs that were holding me back occurred around a situation with my father. My father resigned from his job to pursue a dream business opportunity that unfortunately, did not work out as planned. I clearly remember the devastation in his voice when he told me. I remember feeling how broken his spirit was, and it was during that call that I chose to internalize and interpret the same lesson for myself. I decided that if I were to quit my job to start my own business, I would fail. I decided that I don't come from a family of entrepreneurs and that if I took a risk to start my own business, I would not succeed. This decision became my limiting belief that was still playing out and holding me back on a subconscious level. Whenever I took a step forward in my business, I would subconsciously self-sabotage my efforts. I would start a project but never finish it because, deep down in my subconscious mind, I believed I would fail. My next mental pattern would then play out beating myself up emotionally for not following through on my commitments. It was a vicious cycle to be so motivated to succeed and make a difference in the world, yet feel emotionally handicapped to execute my dreams. I decided and declared after this trauma release process that I would become a successful entrepreneur because it was my choice and I had the power to make my dreams come true.

In addition to my traumas, I was the woman who had ambitious hopes and massive dreams that got sidetracked throughout my life. I put my dreams on hold because I was so busy taking care of my job, my kids, my husband, my parents, my friends, my household, and every other thing or person except for me. I was guilty of negotiating my dreams away from myself by prioritizing and believing everyone else needed to be taken care of before myself. After a few unhealthy work environments and a toxic working relationship, I stopped believing in myself and eventually lost my confidence.

Then one day, I woke up and looked in the mirror and realized I didn't even recognize the person staring back at me. Who was this woman in the mirror? Who was this person I had become? I realized the powerful, confident, and radiant person I used to be slowly drifted away, one decision at a time, only to be left standing there staring at an unloved stranger. This stranger felt unloved and empty because she was too busy pleasing the people around her. She let her validation come from others because she felt like their happiness was more important. If they were happy, then she would be happy. This became a merry-go-round of emotions that she could no longer ride.

So I decided to own what happened to the woman I saw staring back at me. I—*and only I*—had the power to create a new version of myself. I saw the wounded little girl tucked inside of the empty woman staring back at me. I apologized to her for neglecting her and not prioritizing her. I told her I was sorry she didn't feel safe and loved, and I felt bad her happiness had been taken away. I took her little hand and pulled her close. I hugged her so tightly and told her I loved her. I committed to always loving her and promised to protect her and keep her safe. After showing that little girl so much affection, I placed her gently in my heart, and we merged into one. Her happiness was now my priority.

This was a turning point, a realization that it was time to choose me. I could no longer pour from an empty cup. This was my time! I started meditating daily, working out, and creating a network of supportive friends. As I studied Universal Laws, I realized that I was at cause for the effects of my life. I had created all of the positive and negative situations in my life (remove too) based on what I believed about myself. This was a harsh reality to learn. I decided that I would now use the power of the universal laws to create the life I truly desired. I was no longer going to allow the programming I received in my childhood to unconsciously play out in my life. I became committed to my new truths and creating the reality I wanted to experience. I changed my language, healed my traumas, overcame my lack of confidence and codependency, created a new identity, and reprogrammed my mindset to serve me and the achievement of my goals and dreams.

MOVING FORWARD...

My mission is to create a revolution of "Unstoppable Grey". There is a rising tide in grey power as women in their middle ages and beyond who were previously invisible, who had been made to feel less attractive or marketable, are taking back their power. These unstoppable grey women know that these are the best years of their lives. They no longer have young kids at home. They have a new sense of self and are much more confident and clear about who they are and what they want to create in their life. They know the clock is ticking and they have limited time left in this world. They want to be emotionally free to create their dreams and leave their footprint in this world.

If you are tired of taking care of everyone else, feeling like time is fleeting, unsure if you can reach your dreams, feeling stuck in your habits, procrastinating, self-sabotaging, recognizing that you have a problem steeped in the past but unsure of what steps to take to get you out, I can help.

My programs give my clients emotional freedom. I help them figure out what is holding them back. We release their traumas (big and small), energetically cleanse and heal their chakras, birth their life purpose, connect them to their higher self, reprogram their subconscious mind, and I coach them with accountability to obtain the results they desire.

I can help free you from your past traumas. We will create a new mindset that will empower you to get clear on what you want to achieve. Together we can free you from your past traumas. We will create a new mindset that will empower you to get clear on what you want to achieve. We will also create a bulletproof you to become unstoppable in pursuit of a new level of success in your life and business. If you need help with this, please reach out, and let's begin your journey of emotional freedom and entrepreneurial success.

Life Hacks for Entrepreneurial Success

1. You will never achieve the success you truly desire until you believe you are worthy of your dreams. In addition to your professional skill sets, make time to develop a solid foundation of self-love and self-worth so you can be of the highest service to others by aligning your talents, skills, and strengths.

2. Thoughts become things. Your self-image creates your beliefs, which creates your thoughts, which creates the feelings and emotions and the circumstances of your life. See yourself as the eight figure business owner and make decisions from the mindset of this executive.

3. You are your first customer. Prioritize self-care by making time for yourself. Self-care is not just massages and manicures. It is about spending time doing what lights you up and what makes you feel alive. When you are happy, fulfilled, and aligned with your higher self, miracles will happen. You will get the book deal, business funding, or the silent partner you have been searching for.

4. Focus on your frequency. You are not just a body. You emit an energy (an aura) all of the time. It attracts you to the things you desire or the things you do not want in your life. The greatest thing you can

do is put yourself in a frequency of love. When you choose love, things go smoothly in your life. Conversely, when you're in a frequency of frustration, worry, or doubt you will attract more of it. When you are able to stay in love despite being immersed in negative situations, you will become a magnet to incredible power, grace, and peace. Radiate a frequency of iconic success.

5. You are the only thing that can limit you. You are not your limiting beliefs within your subconscious mind. You have the ability to transform your energetics, trauma, and your entire lineage and create the success you desire.

Don't continue to suffer any longer, let's begin your transformation today.

ABOUT THE AUTHOR

ANNE VRYONIDES

Anne Vryonides is a transformational change expert, coach, healer, speaker, and founder of the Freedom Female and the Palm Beach Healing Summit. Anne works with midlife women who are feeling lost in life, stuck, and not achieving the success they desire. Anne left the corporate world a few years back to go on a personal development quest. This journey led her to discover what was holding her back: her subconscious limiting beliefs. Anne now heals and empowers women to transmute their past, realize their power, rewire their brains, and master their emotions so that they can create a new life from the inside out. She is an MBA, NLP master practitioner, RTT practitioner, trauma recovery coach, confidence coach, hypnotherapist, and reiki master.

Anne lives in Florida with her husband, two daughters, and her canine soulmate, Diesel. She loves personal development, traveling, swimming in the ocean, mountain biking, and savoring a chilled glass of Sancerre wine.

Website: https://freedomfemale.com
Instagram: @midlifetransformations

4
HEATHER STEWART

TURNING PAIN INTO POWER

"There's nothing wrong with your daughter," the child psychiatrist reassured my parents. I was 8 years old when I was first put into therapy. Why? Because I was headstrong and independent at a young age. I knew what I wanted and spoke up about it. I was also a normal 8-year-old with normal 8-year-old emotions, which my parents, as with most of their generation, were not equipped to hold space for or help me move through.

Nevertheless, how was this disconnect interpreted by my parents, and what message did I ultimately internalize? Something was wrong with me. I was simultaneously too much because my parents couldn't figure me out and not enough because I wouldn't fit their mold of what a child should be like at 8 years old.

For some context, I grew up in a medical family—my father is a retired cardiothoracic surgeon, my mother a retired neonatal registered nurse, and my sister a neurosurgical physician assistant. You can imagine what dinnertime conversations were like growing up. I'm the firstborn, so you can take a guess at the level of expectations that were placed on me—some might say unreasonably high—and they were imposed at far too young an age. I'll never forget the look of disappointment on my father's face when I got my first B in 7th grade. Imagine the horror when I chose to major in a foreign language at university rather than a scientific or medical field. The nerve!

Having parents with medical professions in America at the end of the 20th century meant that when it came to any medical, psychological, or emotional irregularity, the first, and sometimes only, option considered was the Western medicinal approach—the pharmaceutical one. The possibility that the source could be environmental has never, to this day, been considered. This meant that my siblings and I grew up in a very toxic, emotionally neglectful environment. Mental health issues and addiction are prevalent on both sides of my family, and some of those genes and toxic patterns were passed on to my parents—my father in particular. We were regularly reminded of our shortcomings/inadequacies and rarely celebrated for our accomplishments, even though we each had many. Due to the understandably stressful nature of my father's profession, it was a game of roulette as to what kind of a mood he would be in when he walked through the door every day. And we were expected to tolerate any outbursts of anger and frustration out of "respect". His physical and emotional absence was "typical" for his profession, and we had to learn how to cope. And we did, initiating hypervigilance, people-pleasing, and self-neglect survival mechanisms throughout the rest of the household.

Looking back as a self-aware adult and soon-to-be first-time mother, I know my parents have always done the best they could with what they knew. I'm grateful for all of the opportunities that my father's profession afforded me. I mean, raising children as an emotionally unstable and unavailable person must be extremely difficult. The demand on my father's time and energy to literally save other people's lives meant that our family dynamic looked like this: instead of trying to foster a genuine connection with their children to explore the actual source of our anxiety, depression, and attention deficit disorders, we were pawned off on a throng of medical "professionals", pumped with medications from a young age, and never taught how to regulate our emotions or reconcile our unmet emotional needs because we were often told, "It could be worse. You have everything you need. What is wrong with you?" Yes, we lived a privileged life. We never wanted for anything—save for an emotionally and physically present, accepting, and supportive father. Instead, we were showered with material possessions to compensate for the lack of a gentle, loving parent (I'll let you guess which one of the love languages is NOT how I receive love). Needless to say, I was out of the house at 18.

It didn't end there. It would then take me almost two decades to sort through the subconscious programming that I internalized as a result of my experience growing up with a narcissistic father. I unconsciously perpetuated the same toxic patterns in all areas of my life—relationships with others, my career, my relationship with myself, and even spiritually. After surviving an abusive first marriage (eerily similar to the environment I grew up in), and suppressing that trauma for over a decade, in 2017, the reality of everything I had endured came rushing to the surface in the form of debilitating anxiety and panic.

What was my first move? To see a psychotherapist, of course! I was diagnosed with a panic disorder and put on a cocktail of anti-anxiety medications soon after. [Side note: I'm not knocking pharmaceutical intervention entirely. Medication has its place in a treatment plan, but it's not the end-all, be-all. It is not a solution.] I knew I didn't want to be medicated for life. For this reason, as the good little researcher I was raised to be, I started to explore alternative healing modalities. That's how I found and promptly enrolled in the Institute for Integrative Nutrition's Health Coach Training Program, a program that takes a holistic approach to healing for the mind, body, and soul.

I dove into the program and implemented everything I learned along the way. I saw positive results within a few months. I saw such an improvement in my physical health that I was able to come off all prescription medication entirely. However, I intuitively knew something else was going on at a deeper level. That's when I invested in my first life coach who helped me dig into the uncomfortable, subconscious inner work that I really needed in order to reconcile my childhood trauma with my present reality and toxic patterns.

This was also when I decided to launch my coaching business because the transformation I was seeing in myself was so profound that I knew I now had a responsibility to guide other women with similar struggles. Thus was born Holistic Health 101, my anxiety coaching business. I have made it my mission to use my gifts and experience to positively impact the world by inspiring and empowering women to take control of their lives by digging deep into what is truly holding them back. To guide them along the path towards healing those deep emotional wounds so that they can show up as the confident, unshakeable, unstoppable women they envision themselves to be—the women they already are and just need to reconnect with.

Running your own business is an incredibly humbling experience. And I'm not talking about just the business side of registering, licensing, establishing your practice and processes and such, but more the inner journey of *becoming* a CEO and the deep healing that needs to take place while having no real-world model of what that looks like within the mental health space. Along this entrepreneurial journey, I have come up against so much resistance within myself. Fear, inadequacy, and insecurities I didn't know I had around success, money, and my capability of being a leader and shaker in the mental health industry. I had a lot of healing to do around my limiting beliefs, my identity, and what I thought my business should look like.

The first step in ensuring my success was trusting myself to lead myself through the uncomfortable process of healing the deep emotional wounds that were lurking just under the surface. With every risk I attempted, I would fail—or at least perceive the lack of success as failure. Being raised by a perfectionist meant that I had a deep, visceral fear of failure. I would experience this fear in my physical body so strongly that I couldn't bring myself to sell my services. What if my method doesn't work for some people? What if they think I'm a fraud? Am I really qualified to do this?

What helped me move through these fears? Hiring a coach (or 2 or 3) in addition to my therapist. Having guidance to help me reprogram my beliefs around not only what I want to do but also who I am was the biggest shift in my identity and confidence in my ability to do this important work.

With my coaches' help, I finally figured out that confidence isn't an innate quality. Confident people don't lack fear—they feel it and push through it. Confidence is built by working *through* the discomfort and fear of failure, each time proving to yourself that you *can* do hard things and are phenomenally capable of finding solutions to problems as they arise. It also meant redefining what failure meant to me. It was frustrating at first, especially because no one in my immediate family or social circle understood what I was doing or why.

Nevertheless, I persevered. I anchored myself in my purpose and consistently reminded myself of why I was doing this work. With each new iteration of my programs, with each new attempt to show up, to connect with and provide value to my community, to build my audience, to articulate myself and what I do, and to establish myself as an expert, my confidence grew. I began to see the evidence of my deeper inner healing coming to the surface, and it was creating tangible results—namely, more new clients entering my world every day. My business was finally becoming successful, and it wouldn't have happened had I not done the inner work first.

Since the beginning of my healing journey, I have worked with no less than seven different therapists and coaches on different aspects and levels of my healing. I have tried just about every healing modality—from CBT to NLP to hypnotherapy. I've had such positive results (I am now anxiety-free!) that I have become certified in many of these modalities and incorporate them into my own coaching practice to bring deep, long-lasting healing to women worldwide.

It is through this lens that I would like to share some wisdom with you, my fellow business owner. No matter where you are on your entrepreneurial journey, in addition to the practical and logistical aspects of running a successful business, please consider the inner work that is, in my opinion, far more important than having a snazzy website and gorgeous branding (although, you can have that, too). Here are my secrets to success in any business venture:

COMMIT TO EXPLORING THE UNEXPLORED PARTS OF YOURSELF

Everyone has work to do. We all have shadows we'd rather ignore and allow to exist only behind closed doors. It's easier to avoid and suppress the insecurities, but they will eventually surface. No matter what industry you're in, taking risks will force you to face beliefs and insecurities you didn't know you had. We all want to experience massive success, but in the words of Winston Churchill, "With great power comes great responsibility." Take radical responsibility for uncovering and healing the wounds you need to heal so that you can step into your most confident, empowered self and create the greatest possible impact. For with impact comes success in all forms.

INVEST IN YOURSELF

Hire mentors who currently have what you want—in business, but also emotionally and spiritually. Get into the space and energy of mentors who talk about their struggles openly and who have clear solutions for the obstacles they have overcome that you are currently experiencing. No one enters the entrepreneurial world free from obstacles across all facets of your life and business. Find—and hire—people who offer the right solution for where you are now to help get you to where you want to be.

FAIL ON PURPOSE

You don't start a business knowing exactly what to do to generate incredible wealth and success. You figure it out as you go. In the beginning, this looks like a lot of trial and error. A LOT of failures. But with each perceived failure comes an opportunity to learn, refine, and redirect. Mistakes are invitations for growth. Invite them into your entrepreneurial journey. Don't strive for perfection. Allow yourself to fail on purpose, knowing that you'll come out the other side wiser and with the tools to create the success you envision.

DO IT YOUR WAY

Unlearn everything you learned about what business "should" look, feel, and be like. Thanks to social media and modern technology, you get to decide what business model works for you. You don't have to work 24/7 and exhaust yourself to make the business work—that's an outdated business belief based on toxic productivity. It's time to redefine what success looks like! Find a structure and system that works for you that allows you to create the life you desire—one that is financially lucrative but also allows you time and space to be with family and friends and to be involved with projects that are meaningful to you. Break the mold. Rewrite the script around what a successful business looks like in the 21st century. Even if you're the only one doing it your way, be a leader and an example for others to follow. Chart the path and then teach others how to do the same.

EMBODY YOUR MESSAGE

People are less inclined to hire a mentor or service provider who doesn't practice what they preach. Integrity outweighs knowledge any day. Your business is an extension of yourself and what is important to you. Potential clients and customers can smell inauthenticity a mile away. What's the most attractive quality of an entrepreneur? When they believe so strongly in what they do because they do it/have done it, and they have found—and often created—the best solution to guide others through their respective specialty. BE what you DO. Your people will find you and hire you because you embody what you do at the deepest levels.

OWN YOUR STORY

What is the most powerful selling strategy? Your story. In the age of social media, people want to *feel* something. They want to connect and be moved by your humanity (the triumphs *and* the trials). They want to know they aren't unique in their struggles. They crave to be seen, heard, and made to feel that their obstacles aren't insurmountable. When you tell your truth, you offer that to your community. You create relatability *and* safety—something that is hard to come by in this age of uncertainty. Being vulnerable is scary at first, but it is also liberating and healing for you and your community. Speak your truth, even if your voice shakes. Radical authenticity is the most magnetic force on the planet. People will line up to be in your space *because* of your courage to share your journey with them.

GET READY TO DIVE DEEP!

Each time you experience a deeper layer of healing that requires a new level of growth—and you will because growth and expansion are inevitable—don't shy away from it. Remind yourself that this work is an investment in not only your well-being, but the effects will ripple through your family and community and ultimately create the impact you want in the world. Your commitment to your own healing is helping you break the generational patterns that could be holding you back while simultaneously creating generational wealth and a new paradigm of what success can look like.

As for me, this work has become part of who I am. It is part of my identity at a fundamental level. Through healing myself, I am indirectly healing my family line for generations to come. What's my 'why'? My children and grandchildren will not experience a childhood like mine, so help me God.

Are you with me? Are you ready to turn your pain into power and create your version of success?

ABOUT THE AUTHOR

HEATHER STEWART

Heather Stewart is an anxiety and confidence coach, podcast host, and international bestselling author who works with women to help them overcome anxiety and gain unshakeable confidence so that they can show up powerfully and create the lives that they desire. As a professionally trained educator and health coach, Heather takes a holistic approach to healing, providing a variety of programs and healing modalities for her clients to maximize their results and guarantee their transformation. She has an M.A. in Education and certifications in Integrative Nutrition, Trauma Support Specialist, NLP, Emotional Intelligence, EFT/TFT Tapping, and she's currently pursuing a hypnotherapy certification. She has been featured in ShefNews, Medium.com, Brainz Magazine, Al Kass TV, on several podcasts, and has presented at world-class institutions such as Qatar Foundation.

Heather is from Denver Colorado, USA, and she currently lives in Doha, Qatar, with her husband and their dog, Calvin. She spends her free time traveling, exploring the outdoors, reading, and volunteering in educational, environmental, and animal welfare initiatives.

Instagram: www.instagram.com/_heather.stewart/

5
DR JULIETTE HOBSON

BREATH OF FRESH AIR – A HEALING SUCCESS

I'd like to take you back to the day I had a life-changing moment that I will never forget. As a ten/eleven-year-old, I had difficulties in breathing, and it turned out to be asthma. The only remedies available were nebulisers to help regulate my breathing during asthma attacks and an inhaler to be used daily. I want to share this with you because it's a good opportunity to explain my story and how it led me to become a chiropractor. I'll also give insight into how the body works and whole-body approach tips for an all-encompassing life working from the inside-out.

Sometimes during my preteens I would find myself feeling squeezed around my collar bones and chest—like a vice—and fighting for air. It seemed to happen out of nowhere. It was scary. I would wheeze to the point where I could not breathe in any more oxygen, and later, I'd sit on my own on a nebuliser machine for a boring half-an-hour or until my breathing slowly returned to normal. I had to do this each time it happened. It wasn't a nice experience, and there were times when Mum would have to rush me home from being out on a hobby. Luckily, it never reached a stage where I had to go to hospital. In the beginning, I remember having to breathe into a hard plastic balloon that had the inhaler drug pumped into it, but this wasn't enough and so I was given a nebuliser machine where I used to insert the drug capsule and breathe through a tube until I could breathe normally. That's how it was—and it happened multiple times! Something so fundamental to life, inhaling and exhaling, was being taken away from me. Looking back, this was frightening.

By chance, Mum decided to take me to a chiropractor she had heard about through a friend. We drove about an hour to get there, and I remember standing up to be tested and treated. The chiropractor made some very gentle contact in the centre of my back for barely a moment. He then checked the strength of my arms by asking me to hold my arm out straight to the side and horizontal to the floor and then push up towards the ceiling. At times during the test, my arm would go uncontrollably weak, but it regained strength after treatment. He explained to me that chiropractic "*gives the body the stimulus to allow it to heal itself*". As a 13-year-old, that stuck with me.

The effect of the chiropractic was amazing. That night, I slept on my back—an astonishing change as I usually slept on my front. How incredible! I hadn't even talked about sleeping position in the treatment room and my body naturally changed position, and subconsciously I felt more comfortable sleeping supine. We visited many times. Ultimately, I didn't need to use my nebuliser or any kind of daily or preventer inhaler again.

It was inspiring, to say the least. The chiropractor used to ask what I liked at school and my reply was that I was interested in the body and mind and how it worked. The course for chiropractic was academically intense with a high level of neuroanatomy, anatomy, physiology, pathology, orthopaedics, radiography and radiology along with the practice and art of chiropractic, history of health concepts, demographics and philosophy. If I were going to do it, I would have to work extremely hard.

My passion was ignited, and my academic struggle began. That's what drove me to study biology and chemistry at A-level as they were prerequisites. The minute details of chemistry I found incredibly hard to fathom and remember, and it knocked me so much although my love of human and animal behaviour was always there. I opted to study Psychology at university as I wanted to have a broader view of a person and have fun at the same time. The topics seemed to fit me better in my second and third year, being more cognitive, and I flourished in gaining my degree. Then came the decision of what to do for my career. The chiropractic flame was still there, burning brighter than for anything else, so I applied. After an interview with a lovely lady, I was accepted and offered a place on the course in Bournemouth.

The AECC college was the first one to form in Europe. Since it wanted to set the bar high for others, I gained by going through the most rigorous scientific chiropractic training in the world. I reached my academic pinnacle by getting a first-class honours in my fourth-year project. My chosen subject involved testing haptic perception (sense by touch) in chiropractic students. Touch acuity on the fingertips significantly improved from the first to the fifth year of study. This may seem dull at first but the underlying structural change that takes place is called neuroplasticity. The implications of neuroplasticity are huge, and it refers to the formation of new connections between nerves. You may know of, for example, deaf people having more acute sight and blind people having more acute hearing than people of sight and sound. Neuroplasticity is so exciting! After gaining a Bachelor of Science in human sciences, the reward was to shift into applying my knowledge in a clinic in my fifth year. There was a lot of learning and perseverance involved, and I enjoyed being with the patients. Finally, after a long slog in full-time education, with a Master of Science in chiropractic, I qualified and couldn't quite believe it. It's worth noting that the DC (doctor of chiropractic) after the name of a chiropractor shows they are fully qualified, and this is awarded with post-graduate work while out in practice.

I have steadfastly built my clinical experience by working in clinics as part of a team and on my own. Today I run my own chiropractic practice. I love my work and feel honoured to work with patients from all walks of life. I have helped asthmatics who often come in with mid-back pain or stiffness and I've treated people with all sorts of conditions and all ages, from two weeks to 102 years. Treatment varies depending on history, examination, diagnosis, any other ailments and on what we palpate or find.

INSIDE-OUT TIPS TO HOLISTIC HEALTH:

Chiropractic works from the inside-out so it's more empowering for the patient because it enables the body to naturally regain function. Remember, it gives the body the stimulus to heal itself. Some people may find this a little out in left field. Members of my family, even after I had done my training, were sceptical until they visited a chiropractor themselves. Since my treatment thirty-three years ago, scientific enquiry has proven the change I experienced, and there is plenty of evidence that shows spinal manipulative therapy reducing asthma suffering, sometimes completely. Good scientific discovery is a strict practice. The scientific evidence for chiropractic in general and what we show in clinic is currently based around treating pain, namely, low back pain, migraine prevention, neck aches and joint problems. However, I did *not* go to a chiropractor in pain; this is why it's important to understand that my intention of sharing my story is not purely about me talking about myself. The results were ahead of their time and still are to this day.

The nervous system (brain, spinal cord and nerve supply) is the link between the body function/physiology and the mind/psychology. In recent years, evidence has moved towards showing spinal manipulative therapy changes the neurological or nerve impulses firing to the brain and not just to the spinal cord. In the brain, the area for muscle control has been shown to fire and furthermore receptors in the spine send signals to the brain that change the stress response and affect the equilibrium of biochemicals and hormones in the body that feed the various body systems. Thus, with asthma, the nervous system is stimulated to affect the respiratory system. We still need more randomised controlled trials to be carried out to show the pathways. In my opinion, we need more understanding of the triggers and emotional factors also so as to understand why some come off medication and others don't.

Nutrition is more instrumental in health than exercise—there is a lot of truth in "An apple a day keeps the doctor away". The question is can we eat one apple and be healthy for the rest of our lives? The answer is no; we need to keep working at our health and life each day consistently. While there is some passive genetic immunity, we are not statically immune to disease. Our bodies are finding and processing potential disease-causing cells every second of every day. The body responds to the food we put in it and it's vital to give the body all the nutrients it needs in order for it not to become deficient. I recommend following your instinct and being aware of your cultural flaws and intolerances, which can change over the course of a lifetime. Make sure to include protein when you're looking for a meal. Vitamin B12 is used up a lot in busy lifestyles and B vitamins help form new neural connections but it's more ideal to consume all the vitamins and minerals and cover all bases. Fine-tune your way consistently.

Movement is essential for a healthy body and mind; it isn't only about getting ourselves from one place to another, playing sport, a musical instrument or doing our favourite hobby. As we move, the lymphatic system is affected which is why posture is linked with immunity. We all need to be reminded sometimes that prolonged sitting and sedentary lifestyles are not advised. For those of you who spend much of your day sitting at a desk, it's important to remember to have your workstation set up correctly for your ergonomics and ideally move around for ten minutes in every forty minutes. Whichever type of activity or exercise you choose, it must involve the four Ss: stability, stretch, strength and suppleness. Stability goes hand in hand with good technique, co-ordinating and engaging the right muscles from the upper body and shoulder girdle to the pelvic girdle and lower body. Stretch means flexibility of the whole body by lengthening the muscles. The more flexible we are, the more power we can generate. Strength can be built naturally with exercise and use. Muscle strength helps build bone density too. By suppleness, I mean the softness of a muscle at rest because it is just as important to fully relax a muscle as it is to tense it. Generally physical activities of daily living such as cooking, cleaning, gardening and house renovations are helpful, but if you have overstrained when lifting, been over-bending or moving repetitively in an awkward fashion, this can lead to problems. It is whole body training workouts which are safe and walking in the great outdoors which are beneficial.

Psychosocial aspects account for a large aspect of our lives, whether we believe it or not! The World Health Organisation's definition is 'Health is a state of complete physical, mental and social wellbeing and not merely the absence of disease or infirmity'. Taking time to relax, sleep, do nothing, keep pressure off yourself so you can unwind, along with having the right people around you who support you making decisions about your body are powerful tools. Stress and outside influences will affect us whether we see it or not. Mindset, thoughts and beliefs can also have a role. The definition of intelligence is the ability to adapt so as long as we compensate, we can overcome adversity

I'd like to thank you for reading this. When with my patients or clients, my focus is completely on them, their story, and using my professional knowledge to act in their best interests for what they present with. Self care is about looking after your spine, nervous system and body; We are unable to 'do' chiropractic on ourselves, it can only be done together with another person. My knowledge and expertise can come in handy to help uncover the cause or causes of the pain or dysfunction. Again, neuroplasticity gives hope that we can change and pathways can be re-found or formed for mind and body transformation.

ABOUT THE AUTHOR

DR JULIETTE HOBSON DC

Dr Juliette Hobson DC is a chiropractor who works with people who want to make a difference in their health and wellbeing. They may struggle with an acute episode, chronic condition, have suffered a life event or they may seek facilitation on how to move forward and improve their life and vitality. She helps and empowers them to be at their best mentally and physically. She graduated from Anglo-European College of Chiropractic, Bournemouth, UK in 2002. She has a broad experience working in the South of England and she became Senior Associate in London. She has helped hundreds of people; during this time, she aligned her personal life and enjoys spending time with her friends. She has started up her own practice in Kings Langley, Hertfordshire and lives with her husband, three children and three bunnies.

Facebook: Juliette Hobson Uzur
Instagram: juliette_hobson
Website: juliettehobson.com
Contact to book via Facebook Messenger or Instagram Message

6
KATIE FARRELL

FROM PAIN TO PASSION AND PURPOSE

As I collapsed onto the sofa, completely drained of every last ounce of energy like I'd been unplugged, I knew I just couldn't do this anymore. My mind felt like it had been packed with cotton wool, thoughts seeming to get lost in its woolly mess. Recalling even the simplest of words just felt like too much effort. Something had to change.

Knowing I had only an hour before I had to get up again to collect my son from school brought on a sob of despair.

What was going on?

What was happening to me?

My mind had always been so clear and sharp, yet recently had felt foggy at best and like a load of mush on bad days. I struggled to remember people's names or words mid-sentence and even where I'd parked my car in the multi-storey—something I'd often laughed at family members for doing, when I was renowned for an almost photographic memory.

Even the drive to run the networking groups I managed was being affected. These were meetings I loved! I usually thrived on the energy of the other businesswomen in the room. I loved the support we all gave each other, feeling honoured by the expertise shared and expressed in a truly collaborative, non-competitive way.

But these past few months, I'd found it harder and harder to push through those hours. To stand delivering training. To manage a roomful of women, ensuring everyone had their chance to speak. To share insights or ask questions. It felt like wading upstream through a river of treacle, every movement an effort: muscles feeling like jelly, joints in pain, mind struggling to remember what came next.

It was difficult to understand what was happening from an overall health perspective and how dramatically my energy levels were being impacted.

As a complementary therapist, hypnotherapist and coach, I understood the connection between mind, body and soul and how normally, doing something we love feels easy. We're in flow and there's no effort needed. Time flies when you're having fun, right?

I loved running these meetings and was proud of having established a new franchise territory in my home county, which was really starting to grow and thrive. So why did this now feel like such hard work?

I'd visited my GP several times over the last few years, as the variety of symptoms—migraines and, most disturbing of all, sudden fainting episodes—I was experiencing had been increasing in number and frequency as well as intensity. Yet despite various tests and scans, they couldn't find any specific medical causes and so eventually diagnosed ME/Chronic Fatigue Syndrome and Fibromyalgia, for which there are no known treatments or cures in the medical world; you're just told to take pain killers and bed rest for the fatigue. As a single parent running two businesses with the only support being from my parents, who were in their early 70s, I didn't know whether to laugh or cry! If only they could prescribe someone to run my businesses, do the ten school runs and housework every week so I could get the bed rest!

And so I did what I've always done; I dug a little deeper into my reserves (which were little more than fumes by this stage) and took the difficult decision to sell my networking franchise. It was so tough because, not only does your own business feel like your baby that you've nurtured and watched grow from day one, but also I've always lived by the ethos of: "If something's worth doing, it's worth doing well".

I felt a huge responsibility to my members too. Yet I knew that, in order to be truly supportive of them and their businesses, I had to hand the reins over to someone else who had the time and energy to dedicate to them. And the power of a network really came into its own when I was introduced to a lovely woman through a mutual contact. It was with mixed emotions that I 'handed over the keys' to the new owner; however, I've always been very intuitive and found that any decisions I made following my heart/gut instinct had worked out well—and this certainly felt like the right way to go.

Over the next year, I managed my health and responsibilities as best I could by taking on some associate coaching contracts where I only had to work 1-2 days per week and just covered my outgoings. This schedule enabled me to rest as much as possible on the other days and be there as a mum for my son.

I tried various therapies to treat the conditions, to varying degrees of success, plus any relief they provided seemed only temporary. I was a qualified massage therapist, reflexologist and Reiki Master myself, and I believe these tools certainly helped prevent me from truly crashing into fully bed-ridden states I'd read of others suffering and enabling me to have days when I could get up and work. But sometimes, self-treatment just felt too hard!

I also did lots of research into ME/Chronic Fatigue and Fibromyalgia; all are sadly much more common than I'd realised, and whilst there are some suggestions for treating the symptoms, there didn't seem to be any known cure.

Another impact of these truly debilitating conditions is the additional stress they cause. In addition to the symptoms and financial worries, the indirect stress from lack of physical exertion was just as awful.

I've always been very active, from being on every sports team at school, doing ballet for 10 years and taking classes in everything from yoga and Pilates to kickboxing training and salsa dancing. For me, exercise isn't just about the physical activity; it's also an outlet for emotional and mental stress. There's no better way to get stuff out of your system than shaking your hips on the dancefloor or throwing some jabs at a punchbag! But having CFS and Fibromyalgia meant that I either didn't have the energy to do any exercise, or on the odd day that I did, I would pay for it with a fatigue crash, feeling like I had the flu and been run over by a steam roller, anything from 1-3 days later with no apparent pattern. My life felt out of control; I couldn't even plan for the good or the bad days, not knowing when they'd occur. I became very good at fixing a smile on my face and 'pulling up my big girl pants' to get through work, only to collapse in a heap for hours afterwards. And I knew that not only was this no way to live, I simply couldn't sustain it for much longer.

It was in the summer of 2019 when things finally started to shift. I came across a post on Facebook from a couple called Liv & Raf of 5th Dimension Earth. I was aware of Liv as a fellow member of an online global networking group and had seen some of her energy healing sessions there. Now here they were, posing the simple question: "What do you think your soul purpose is?"

Even though I'd seen versions of this question posed countless times before—like many of us, I'm sure—there was something about this one that demanded I stop scrolling and respond. I wasn't expecting anything from it at the time; I just remember posting my response and enjoying reading others' replies.

A few days later, I saw Liv and Raf doing a livestream to provide spiritually guided feedback to everyone. Well, this had me hooked now! Over the years and through various personal experiences, including the birth of my son, qualifying as a Reiki Master, and many more, I was aware of what I referred to as having strong intuitive and healing abilities. However, throughout my earlier 20-year career in the corporate world, I'd pretty much kept these to myself. I'd worked mainly in the male-dominated IT field and could only imagine how sharing them might have gone down!

Now, the opportunity to learn further insight seemed far too good to miss. So, I tuned in, and on hearing my feedback, whilst I didn't understand the full implications at the time, it just felt so true. It really hit home, and I just knew I had to discover more. The only way I can describe the feeling was like emerging from a dense jungle you've been lost in for ages and someone handing you a torch, with the offer of a map to follow.

What happened over the next couple of years went beyond words, and I could probably fill at least two entire books with all the experiences and expansions I went through. However, one of the most impactful for me was going through a spiritual awakening and discovering an abundance of energetic healing capabilities that I'd previously only tapped into a fraction of. They have been described since as like a combination of Reiki & Hypnotherapy on steroids!

Through an intensive process of discovery about our souls, spiritual Guides, my individual purpose and energetic capabilities, I began to understand that everything my life had comprised of up to this point —my natural strengths, values, desires and experiences (good and bad!), together with the qualifications such as CBT-Hypnotherapy, sports hypnosis, personal development coaching, Reiki and neuroscience amongst others—had all been for a reason and the pieces of the jigsaw were starting to fall into place.

I learnt that I came here to be a powerful healer, to help free others from the shackles that are restricting them from fulfilling their potential and living the life they came here for. The huge, positive ripple effects I could envision happening across the world ignited something in my soul, and I just knew I had to take this further!

So, I set about understanding and developing these energetic skills further. One of these uses a combination of energetic 'tools' that enables me to connect with another person and tune into their conscious, subconscious and unconscious minds to uncover any experiences from their past that had been traumatic for them, whether emotionally, mentally, physically or energetically.

When we go through trauma, or a negative experience, especially if we're too young to understand, express or deal with the impact of it, the memory can get hidden or locked away deep in our subconscious/unconscious as a means of self-protection so that we don't keep remembering and reliving it. However, this doesn't prevent the memory from being re-triggered by subsequent events of a similar nature. So this re-triggering can continue well into adulthood, manifesting as any number of challenges from psychological issues to physical illness.

I started by practising on myself and focusing on the CFS and Fibromyalgia I was still struggling with.

I was able to recall experiences from my past that had been the initial cause of trauma and which I'd completely forgotten about and subsequent memories where the emotions I'd experienced were similar to those from the original event.

To give you some background, all emotions are energy (everything in the Universe is energy-based) and have their own vibrational frequency. Positive emotions, such as love, peace, gratitude and joy, vibrate at a higher frequency, whilst negative emotions, such as anger, grief and fear, vibrate at much lower frequencies. If you're aware of The Law of Attraction (just one of many Universal Laws of Energy), you'll know that like energies (or vibrations) attract like energies.

To expand on this, if we have a traumatic experience but don't release the energy of it from our bodies, the resulting low vibrational energy can get trapped and over time attract further low-frequency energies, accumulating into large stores of low vibration energy, right down to a cellular level. Depending on where in the body they get stored, these energies can develop into physical injuries, health conditions or mental blocks and limitations. These can manifest as anything from Imposter Syndrome, a weak ankle joint or even cancer.

In my case, the trauma had caused a decline in my immune system, eventually allowing the virus Glandular Fever to get in (I contracted this at age 19). Because the trauma was left unresolved, it got re-triggered over the following years, causing the trapped low energies to grow and further impact my immune system, lymphatic and muscular skeletal systems, developing into the long-term syndromes of CFS and Fibromyalgia.

I received insight into many other impacts, including on my heart, the causes of brain fog and reduced function of the mitochondria (the energy-generating parts of all cells), which led to a lot of the fatigue I experienced. All of this explained the debilitating symptoms I'd been struggling with for so long.

I was then guided to perform specific energy healing on myself, targeting all of the issues identified and received guidance that the healing would take just a few weeks to complete.

At that point, I didn't really know what to expect; however, whilst the improvements started happening gradually over the coming days, I can still remember vividly the point at which I knew it had worked. I was standing at the sink one evening, washing up, and I remember thinking, "I'm so tired; I can't wait to finish this and get to bed!" In the next instant, it hit me. I knew with absolute certainty that the type of tiredness I was experiencing was 'normal'; the type that everyone faces when they've done a bit too much through the day, and that after a night's sleep, I would wake the next day feeling rested and ready to go again. This wasn't the bone-aching, utter fatigue I'd become accustomed to, where no amount of sleep seemed to make any difference to the exhaustion that consumed me.

I remember laughing out loud at the realisation! I wasn't entirely sure how I knew; I just did, and I couldn't wait to get in bed and have a good sleep to prove it to myself...which I absolutely did!

From then on, it was as if someone had flicked a switch in my mind and body. I noticed my mind felt clearer than it had in a long time, and getting up in the morning was no longer a painful process. I could go a whole day without falling asleep, and I generally had more energy than I'd experienced for years!

I also became acutely aware of just how many other people were experiencing similarly debilitating conditions and how I wanted the same huge transformation for them that I'd had.

The words of Liv and Raf in their livestream came back to me stronger than ever: "You came here to be a powerful healer".

I'd also received insight from my own Spiritual Guides that I was to be "a leader that guided others to their own purpose and fulfilment," and now I could truly believe this; I'd seen and felt the evidence with my own eyes, mind, body and soul!

And so started the next chapter of my life.

I've worked with lots of people already to help them heal from various challenges, including CFS/ME, chronic back pain, hormonal imbalances and Covid/long Covid. I even helped a GB tri-athlete compete at the 2022 World Championships after she'd suffered an auto-immune response to the Covid vaccinations, causing many old injuries to flare up. Her doctors had advised her to give her body 18-24 months to deal with it as there was nothing they could do—time she just didn't have if she wanted to achieve her dream of competing.

There are also the mental and emotional impacts that clients experience in their work and their relationships. Helping them discover their own sense of purpose and developing their gifts is priceless.

I can't express enough how grateful I am for this journey I've been on. Without the challenges I've faced, I wouldn't have had such a deep understanding of the truly debilitating impacts our life experiences can have on us—be they psychological, emotional, physical or energetic—both personally and professionally. It's connected me with so many amazing people all over the world, and to know that I can now help others to heal, find their purpose and go on to create lives they love and feel a sense of freedom in, for me, is the greatest gift that I'm passionate about sharing with the world.

As Oprah Winfrey said:

"There is no greater gift you can give or receive than to honour your calling. It's why you were born. And how you become most truly alive."

If, through sharing my personal journey from pain to passion and purpose, I inspire hope in just one person currently experiencing pain, that there can be so much more joy, ease and freedom for them, I'll be happy!

For now, from one entrepreneur to another, here are some learnings I'd love to share with you:

1. Trust yourself. Our gut instincts are our inner satellite navigation systems, so if yours tells you something feels great, or not, follow its guidance; I guarantee you won't regret it!

2. When the going gets tough, remember these words from US writer Susan L Taylor: "In every crisis there is a message. Crises are nature's way of forcing change – breaking down old structures, shaking loose negative habits so that something new and better can take their place."

3. Build a Network. The life of an entrepreneur can be a lonely place, so having a network of like-minded people around you can help you make great connections on both a business and personal level.

4. It's not just OK to ask for help; it's practically imperative! We can't expect to know everything about running a business. By investing in support from a mentor, coach or other expert who has either been where you are and can share their wisdom, or can guide you through the tough times and celebrate your successes with you, you can save so much time, money and energy.

ABOUT THE AUTHOR

KATIE FARRELL

Katie Farrell is a high performance coach helping high achieving women and athletes to play at their best, achieve their best and feel at their best without burnout or sacrifice. She takes a fully integrated approach incorporating the physical, mental, emotional, and spiritual aspects of the human, so they can achieve the success they desire, being unapologetically all woman, in a way that feels good.

Website: www.katiefarrell.co.uk
LinkedIn: www.linkedin.com/in/katiefarrellcoach/

7

KELLY TAN

YOU ARE YOUR SUPERPOWER

"There is no one else like you." - KT

In an instant, my life was turned upside down. Never did I think this could happen to me. I couldn't breathe, and all I saw was darkness. My life was over as I knew it. I dropped to my knees and wept.

What has just happened? This can't be happening. Surely, it is just a nightmare. But it wasn't. My marriage had just failed.

Flashback to a few years ago: I reached my breaking point when the demands from my beauty salon business tipped me over the edge, and I knew I had to make a change.

Although it was the most difficult decision to make, I sold my business to allow myself to spend more time with my family. I needed to be fully present in my child's important moments—first steps, first words, and first days of school.

My business had been born out of passion and hard work. Under my leadership, we won multiple awards and were named in the Top 10 Nail Salons. The salon quickly became a household name for the best nail and waxing services.

However, it came to a point where what was once my passion became something I dreaded every day.

After selling the salon, I never felt happier. The weight that had been pressing down on my shoulders for what felt like an eternity finally lifted.

But that happiness ended shortly after that, when my marriage failed.

I had no idea how I would make ends meet or how my little one would grow up, thrive, and develop through such difficult circumstances. It was the most devastating and challenging time of my life, but I had to be strong for the both of us.

I set out on a journey of self-discovery to gain clarity on who I was and what I wanted in life. I pushed myself beyond my limits, learning new things and discovering hidden talents along the way. It was challenging but immensely fulfilling, and it motivated me to start an online business where I could put my focus on creating a better life for myself.

FAILURE

Although I had parted ways with my business, my passion for nails had never left. And as if a lightbulb had gone off in my head, the idea of teaching nail technicians worldwide how to create Japanese nail art developed. I regained the fire in my belly and immediately got to work. And thus came about my first online business: a nail membership for nail technicians.

My parents taught me to *never* give up, and I thank them for constantly supporting me in this journey that led to what I've achieved today.

I spent a few months working tirelessly, building the site and creating content. I recorded and edited tutorials, prepared and planned a launch, and created content for social media—all by myself.

I felt on top of the world, like I could conquer anything. I had never been prouder of myself.

But that fire was soon snuffed after the membership site launched and not a single person signed up. It took me a while to come to terms with the crushing disappointment of failure. I couldn't have felt more disappointed in myself.

Since I was unemployed and had no income, I decided to look for a job to support myself. My job search quickly led to a Social Media Manager position in a media agency, and although the income was a significant drop from what I was earning prior, I was dead-set on learning and developing my skills.

> *"Greatness is born out of believing in yourself. Once you have that, nothing can stop you." - Anonymous*

This experience taught me the processes and systems behind a successful social media agency. I saw how a team of people with different skill sets came together to produce creative and effective content for their clients.

I thoroughly enjoyed my time there and the opportunity to meet so many amazing and interesting people but...

THE TURNING POINT THAT CHANGED EVERYTHING

Nine months later, I was suddenly made redundant. Although I was always one of the most hardworking, responsible, and reliable employees, my role was suddenly deemed redundant because the agency was forced to cut back on costs and reduce expenses.

What now? The question echoed in my mind.

I joined a few freelance platforms, taking all the skills and experience I gained from working at an agency, and started offering social media management services. This allowed me to use my creativity and knowledge to help businesses grow their online presence.

That entrepreneur in me didn't die. I knew I was born for greatness. Along the way, I discovered my true passion in life.

SURRENDER TO MY SOUL'S CALLING

I found immense joy in helping business owners market their businesses on social media.

The first few months were tough because most clients on these platforms wanted highly experienced freelancers but at the lowest rate.

I had my fair share of nightmare clients, but I was up for the challenge. The biggest lesson I learned from owning a beauty salon was patience, having dealt with a customer base that demands patience and attention to their requests and needs.

> *"Your greatest comeback is just around the corner." - Anonymous*

I quickly amassed an impressive portfolio of clients. I worked hard and rose through the ranks, becoming one of the top-rated freelancers. I was invited to join an elite group of top talent on the portal, where we got to work with high-profile clients, some of whom I still work with.

Although things were looking up for me in my career, I was still struggling to get by...

HEALING THE WOUNDS & THE ROAD TO RECOVERY

I was still recovering from the shock of a failed marriage when I decided to move to Australia. It has always felt like home, and I was hoping a fresh start would help me heal and move on.

In November 2019, I arrived in Melbourne with my little one in tow with one suitcase each and our hand-carry luggage. I remember that sunny morning as if it was just yesterday. My little one was sitting on one of the luggage, waiting for our ride. He gave me the biggest smile, and I instantly knew everything would be okay.

Even though I had spent a reasonable amount of time in Melbourne, relocating was still scary. This time, it wasn't just me; I had a dependant, and life was going to be very different from what it was before.

The first few months in Australia were really tough. I was homesick and missed my parents, but I was determined to make the most of my new surroundings.

I was going through many emotions, still recovering from the shock of a failed marriage. All the while, I was juggling work and client meetings. In the presence of my little one, I was that happy mom who gave it her all; when my little one was in school, I could allow myself to cry and eventually heal.

Healing and putting the pieces of my life back together again took time. The heartbreak was a significant block; at times, I felt I could never move on. However, I was lucky to have a strong support system in my friends and family, who helped me through the tough times and constantly reminded me of how amazing I am.

I found comfort in journaling and working out, which allowed me to process my thoughts and feelings more constructively. Getting regular exercise also helped to boost my energy and mood.

It was a long and difficult process, but with time, I healed.

Looking back on what happened in the past few years, I can see the pathway to my success. It prepared me for challenges. I never knew I had the strength in me to overcome obstacles one after another, whether in business or personal life.

ACHIEVING SUCCESS

From a physical store owner to a purely online, remote business.

"I am born a fighter." - Anonymous

I founded Kelly Talks Social, a business with a vision and mission of helping women entrepreneurs market their businesses online through my private and group coaching container, podcast, courses, digital products, online community, and done-for-you marketing.

My mission now is to help women in my community take their businesses to a whole new level of success—**zero to abundance**. My goal is to help them achieve independence, financial freedom, and abundance so they can live a stress-free life and, most importantly, earn with ease.

Success is what you perceive it to be, not necessarily related to money or material things. Success can be any of these:

- Your side hustle becoming your main hustle,
- Stepping out of your comfort zone to pursue what you enjoy,
- Moving on from a toxic relationship,
- Helping people in some way, shape, or form.
- What's yours?

> *"I've been broken before, but it did not deter me from achieving success." - KT*

My success was being able to pivot a business amidst the chaos and turmoil in my life. Not only did I survive, but I thrived through challenging times and emerged stronger than ever before.

Now, I can enjoy freedom in business and life by doing what I love every day, allowing me to live fearlessly and independently on my terms, to the fullest, and in the present.

These days, my life looks a little something like this: client meetings, coaching calls, content creation, launching programs, collaborating with like-minded individuals, and meeting new friends. It's all fun without the burnout and living a life by design.

Most importantly, happiness is the core of success that led the way. Everything else that comes along is a bonus.

How did I go from a burnt-out heartbroken business owner to the successful woman I am today?

I'm sharing my story to inspire and empower you to pursue your dream.

Now, I'm spilling my secrets to success, sharing the life-changing wisdom that I know will help you thrive. I am opening up about everything I've learned over the years, offering you a pathway to achieving your dreams and success.

ENTREPRENEUR SUCCESS SECRETS

Secret #1 Mindset

Mindset is everything. A strong foundation is key for any building—it's what allows it to stand tall and weather even the strongest storms. The same principle applies to entrepreneurship. You need a strong foundation to withstand the ups and downs of your business.

Growth versus fixed mindset, which one are you? Be a lifelong learner. A fixed mindset will keep you in your comfort zone, while a growth mindset will push you to take risks and continually learn and adapt.

The most important thing is to remind yourself that your mindset is a choice, and it's up to you to decide whether you want to remain stuck or continue growing.

Your mind is incredibly powerful, yet it cannot differentiate between what's real and what's not. The power of visualization helps you achieve your goals by conditioning your mind to see, hear, and feel success. That is why it is important to think positively and act as if you are living THAT life. It is up to you to create the outcome that you want.

Secret #2 Grit, Perseverance & Resilience

These are key characteristics for anyone who wants to be successful. It's what makes you determined to bounce back from failures and setbacks.

For entrepreneurs, the initial startup stage is an exciting time: you're passionate about your idea and dedicated to building the business. Your energy is at an all-time high.

The reality is that there are highs and lows in any business. When you hit a low, it can be tough to stay motivated and engaged, but this is when you need to persevere, remind yourself that you're in this for the long haul, and keep going no matter what.

When you keep your eye on the finish line, it's easier to push through the valleys and enjoy the peaks. Think of your business as a marathon, not a sprint.

Secret #3 Face Your Fears

If you want to grow and achieve great things, you have to be willing to face your fears and embrace stepping out of your comfort zone. That's where the real magic happens.

Every person has fears that dominate their thoughts and restrict their life. Some of these fears, such as fear of failure, rejection, or success, are common. Other fears are less common but no less powerful.

Overcoming your fears is a huge part of being a successful entrepreneur. Just like any other obstacle, it's something that you need to learn how to conquer.

While you can't completely remove fear, you can and should learn how to overcome it. One way to do this is by reframing your thoughts. Don't be afraid to take risks and put yourself out there. You might just surprise yourself with what you're capable of achieving.

Secret #4 Health

You must prioritize your health. Physical fitness is one of the keys to a successful entrepreneurial career. Just as athletes need to be physically fit to perform at their best, entrepreneurs need to be physically and mentally fit to withstand the demands and challenges of business.

Burnout is a real problem for entrepreneurs. My biggest mistake was not prioritizing exercise, so I burnt out in my twenties. Now, my daily morning routine includes exercise, a non-negotiable.

Secret #5 Commitment

Entrepreneurship isn't for the faint-hearted. It takes immense hard work and dedication to get your business off the ground and even more to keep it running. Successful entrepreneurs are always committed to their businesses.

This is what drives entrepreneurs to continue working towards their goals even when things are tough, and it's what sets them apart from people who only dream about starting a business.

One thing that kept me going was looking back at my purpose and my why. I have the power to make a difference.

Secret #6 Take Action

Have you ever purchased an online course but not taken any action and made zero progress? Inaction is the barrier to your success.

Too often, people tend to intellectualize information instead of taking the required action immediately. Learning is great, but successful results are created by taking massive and consistent action.

. . .

Secret #7 Find A Mentor

Mentors are a must-have in any entrepreneur's toolbox. They motivate you through actionable guidance and resources. You can learn from their previous mistakes and successes.

Find a mentor that can help you achieve your goals quicker. Draw on the expertise of someone who has already achieved what you're striving for.

Every successful entrepreneur has a mentor or coach to help them stay focused and guide them through their journey to success. It's time you find one now.

What I'm doing now is just the tip of the iceberg. My aim is to speak on world stages to inspire and empower women worldwide to chase after their dreams and create their financial independence with joy and confidence.

This is only a chapter of a story of a woman who rose from the darkness, reconstructed her path, and redefined success.

FINAL WORDS

I want to leave you with this:

You are the driver of your destination. Whether you step on the brakes or accelerator to keep going is up to you.

Success is what you make of it. It's the sum of your efforts, choices, and willingness to persevere through difficult times. It's a measure of how well you've navigated life's challenges and accomplished your goals.

You hold the power to unlock and unleash the greatness in you and soar higher.

Keep shining bright.

Believe you can, and it will happen.

ABOUT THE AUTHOR

KELLY TAN

Kelly Tan is the founder of Kelly Talks Social and has over 10 years of marketing and social media experience. She is a Social Media & Content Coach who helps coaches and service providers market their business on social media. Kelly was driven by the need to help business owners grow online, be more visible, get more clients and earn with ease. Her mission is to inspire and empower women entrepreneurs to rise up, create their own independence and freedom in business and in life. Kelly has helped many business owners with proven strategies and tools to turn their business from zero to abundant. She helps through 1:1 coaching, online courses, and digital products. She was a former beauty salon owner of 10 years who built a multi-award-winning salon through the power of social media. Her book Success Codes - Secrets You Weren't Taught In School is an international award-winning bestseller on Amazon. She is a certified marketer, nail technician, waxing therapist, barista, and a foodie. Kelly lives in Melbourne, Australia.

Website: kellytalkssocial.com/
Instagram: www.instagram.com/kellytalkssocial/
Facebook: www.facebook.com/kellytalkssocial

8

KIMBERLY J BENOIT

WHAT ARE YOU WAITING FOR?

MY STORY

I wish I could say I had this lightning bolt moment when I just knew I wanted to run my own business as a leadership coach and consultant. I didn't. My life simply hasn't been ... well, that simple.

I found myself in my early 40s, newly divorced and hating life. I was floating in my corporate career. When I looked in the mirror, I didn't know who was staring back at me anymore. For so long, I had just been taking what was offered in life or doing what needed to be done to survive versus asking for what I wanted. But let's be honest, I didn't even know what I wanted or who I was at this point.

All I knew was I felt unfulfilled and there had to be more in life than this. At one time, I had been a young, vivacious woman out to set the world on fire, but somewhere along the way I got lost in who I thought I was supposed to be. Compromising on what I wanted to make my career and marriage work. Suddenly after divorce, the 'we' had now become just me. It was now up to me to regain a fulfilling life.

Facing this personal and professional crossroads, I had a choice to make. I could continue to climb someone else's ladder, which was what I'd been successfully doing for quite some time, or I could take a step back and really figure out who I was and what I wanted, and more importantly, why I wanted it.

One of the smartest and most pivotal investments in myself during those challenging years was working with two professional coaches, Nancy and Allyson. By golly, these ladies were some firecrackers and really challenged me to see myself more clearly. They challenged the stories I told myself and didn't allow me to play the victim. Even though I worked with Nancy in 2018 and worked with Allyson in 2020, the conclusions and trends were the same.

I had completely lost touch with what my heart was trying to tell me because I was so deep in my head. I was trying to make it all make sense and have a plan for everything. By overthinking, I was almost inevitably killing any creative spark or risky idea to shake up my world. Ultimately, I was talking myself out of considering or pursuing things that were good for me because I was scared.

A hard lesson for me to learn was to let go and start listening to my heart because it was going to tell me where to go—even if it was just baby steps. The truth is, they were right.

What I didn't realize in these moments was that I was learning to trust myself. My little inner voice. Each step forward was laying the foundation for greater change to come.

It led me to traveling and to begin to really embrace things that just brought me joy. And ever so slowly, that spark of joy became a blazing fire. It became very clear to me I was selling myself short. I was creating limitations and hurdles by overthinking and underestimating who I was and what I had to offer the world.

So let me take a step back and tell you a bit about who I am. I have had the most amazing life, having worked for Fortune 20 companies to small nonprofits. I have worked with individuals and teams through major changes, creating strategies and plans to successfully navigate challenges. I have worked with hundreds of individuals across various industries, helping them figure out how to navigate moments in their lives and careers. In essence, helping others get out of their way on the path to fulfillment and success.

Somehow, because I was so lost in my head, I believed I didn't have it in me to be my own boss or to plot my own course. I clearly could not coach myself as I doubted I was good enough to do it on my own. How crazy is that?!? With the breadth of all I had done and experienced in life, I was the perfect person to truly create a business in the service of others.

Working with these two coaches truly ignited in me something that forever changed the course of my life. I guess it technically started with my divorce, but without the self-reflective work I did with them, I was forced to face the reality that the only person holding me back was myself. I had to create and chase my dreams.

Another theme that arose from my coaching work was to consider becoming a certified coach myself. With my background and experience, coaching came naturally to me, and I really liked the idea of helping others as I had been helped.

After a lot of self-doubt and questioning whether I was good enough and rethinking all the old stories to talk myself out of trying something scary, I bit the bullet and signed up for an ICF training program. I decided to invest in myself and knew it would tell me if this was the way to go.

You know what? Spoiler alert. It absolutely was the right decision.

I had a few final shoves into going out on my own. First, I reconnected with an old classmate who happened to be doing executive coaching herself. Her support furthered the feeling in my heart and soul that I was taking steps in the right direction. Again, another sign.

The final tipping point was when I attended a women's leadership retreat. A big part of their process was providing feedback and, I know you're going to find this hard to believe but, the same messaging came back to me. I heard Nancy's and Allyson's words echoing all around me. "What are you waiting for?" and "You have it in you to follow your dreams."

All I could think was, "Well, Universe, I'm paying attention. You've been sending the message over and over again with different messengers, and I promise I'm hearing this time." And boy, did I take a leap.

If the pandemic taught us anything ... tomorrow is never guaranteed. So, get out there and live the life you want to live. Your dreams, like mine, are not crazy; they are attainable. It does take a lot of courage to step out of that safe rut you are sitting in.

After all the years of people I trusted telling me the same thing, I am happy the message really sunk in. Some (like my mother) might call it hardheadedness, but I prefer to think I was just reflecting and refining my options. Like a fine wine, some things just need a little more time.

Ultimately, I decided that I had to believe in me. Period.

And guess what? I knew that I could do this. With the support of my family, friends, and professional network, I had all the support and experience needed to be successful. I just needed to take the first step.

And guess what happened when I did? I had things to learn and mistakes to make, but I didn't allow there to be an alternative. I was tired of being tired of a life I didn't want. I wanted a different life and have made choices to achieve my attainable goals. It just required courage.

Today, I work with the most amazing individuals and teams across the United States and help them navigate their fears and toxic stories and help them become the best person/team that they possibly can be. I am a leadership coach and know that I am making a difference because of who I have been and how I bring my experience to the table. All of those trying moments make me a better coach and consultant for those that I serve. I am able to humbly and compassionately meet everyone where they are along the challenging journey of leadership and life and support them in being the leader they want and know that they can be. This is my differentiator. No one can help them the way that I can.

Along this journey, here are a few things that have helped me navigate the transition and supported me along this path. I am happy to share these with you, hoping they might also help you.

MY GUIDANCE

1. Create a personal mission statement.

The journey of entrepreneurship can be long and lonely. Sometimes you will question what you are doing and whether this is the right path. One way I have kept myself focused is by creating my very own mission statement.

Companies have them as a guiding light, sharing to the world why they are here and what value they provide. If they have one, why shouldn't we?

Take your time and really write it out. It doesn't have to be fussy or fancy. Just simple words. Mine is more of a collection of phrases that are meaningful to me. Here it is:

Pursuing connection with others, enlightened by life, driven by integrity & purpose, honoring the unique perspective & journey of others.

See? Nothing fancy. I have mine printed out and taped to my monitor so I can read it daily. It keeps me grounded and focused on what matters most. When I find my resolve faltering, it is wonderful to be reminded that I am on the right path and living my purpose.

2. Have and use a Board of Directors.

What is a Board of Directors, you ask? It is a group of people that you trust implicitly and seek guidance from. This could include friends and family, but should also include peers, mentors, advisors, and coaches. People who have a genuine interest in your success and will speak truth to you when you are right and, more importantly, when you are off course. The important part is to have a mix of people and to ensure that they aren't all 'yes' people.

Members of this group may stay consistent while others rotate in and out as your life and goals change. You will want some to have industry knowledge to help guide you along your specific path.

This group is there to serve as your critics and advocates. To help you plan. To celebrate with you when milestones are reached and, importantly, to pick you up when there are disappointments. When you struggle, and you will, someone from this group will be a go-to person to talk to and provide a much needed nudge or kick in the pants.

Be open to what they have to tell you. Sometimes they will give you harsh truths that are needed for you to be successful. Despite the sting, you have to know your blind spots to be able to prepare and succeed.

3. Have a plan, but be prepared to pivot.

As a former project manager, I can plan in my sleep. Once I decided that I wanted to pursue an entrepreneurial path, my mind immediately began to create a detailed to-do list. I wanted to make sure I was thinking everything through and creating the best plan possible for how to navigate what I thought might happen.

As with all best-laid plans, they are great to have on paper, but reality proved some of them to be unnecessary, unrealistic or off the mark. Once I left corporate life and fully embraced this new world, I was grateful that I had prepared for what I could. However, many things didn't turn out as I expected. All of those plans needed to be re-evaluated.

The pivots, or other aspects I was unprepared for, included various opportunities that fell into my lap. They weren't part of my plan, but gosh, they got me excited and wasn't this why I wanted a change in the first place? To live more fully and share my gifts with the world.

All of this to say, make some plans. Research and really understand your industry and competition. Know who you are in this space. But once faced with the inevitably unexpected realities of life and business, be prepared to pivot. Trust your gut and follow your fire. You might be surprised that you end up somewhere better than your plan could have ever predicted.

4. Network. Network. Network.

I can't reiterate this one enough. Get out there and meet people in your industry. Even if you are technically competitors, I have found that most people really wanted to help me succeed. This has happened in a variety of ways. For instance, sometimes opportunities present themselves and you know someone else would be a better fit. Helping others be successful puts great karma into the world. More importantly, it shows potential clients that you have their best interests at heart. That matters more than just taking work just to take it, especially if you aren't the right person for the job.

I would also encourage you to network with people outside of your industry. Seek out people you admire and grow those skills that need developing. This is a great way to be innovative and apply different approaches to your business.

Lastly, surround yourself with the most positive people. You want to have folks around you who believe in all that is possible and believe in you too. Keep seeking out these rays of sunshine because that is where the magic happens, when people believe help you see all that is possible.

5. Believe in yourself. Because if you don't, no one else will.

I saved the most important for last. Believe in yourself. Now, for a little reality check, there are days when I don't trust what I am doing or I still get too much into my head. As with anything, it is all a journey. Ride the wave. Read your mission statement. Call someone on your Board of Directors.

You must believe the following with every fiber you have:

- You are good enough today.
- You are worthy now.
- You are here for a reason.
- You have something to offer.

Don't let the dark days steal your light. If you need to, take a day off and start fresh tomorrow. Whatever you do, keep going and stay focused. The world needs your gifts.

CHOOSING MYSELF

I wish I could say that the list above is magical and that every day is filled with rainbows and unicorns. Unfortunately, that isn't true. Some days are great. Others require more self-reflection, self-love, and work. Fortunately, most days are pretty awesome.

I just want to leave you with one final thought. The one truth that has come out of all of this is the possibilities are endless when the greatest limitation—me—is no longer standing in the way.

ABOUT THE AUTHOR

KIMBERLY BENOIT

Kimberly Benoit is a Leadership Coach & Consultant that works with leaders and teams across all industries, but often share a similar challenge of being stuck in toxic or unhealthy patterns, unable to confidently navigate needed change for continued success. Through a compassionate approach, she empowers them to confront the real issues and to create realistic next steps to move forward with confidence. She launched her business after an accomplished 24-year career as strategic and operational leader with expertise in program management, change management, crisis management, strategy development, and organizational effectiveness. Kimberly is active in the Project Management Institute (PMI) and the International Coaching Federation (ICF). She holds advanced degrees in Clinical Psychology and Criminal Justice. In addition, Kimberly is certified in the Mindful Leader's Mindfulness-Based Stress Reduction (MBSR) program and the Harrison Assessment. Kimberly lives in New Orleans, LA and enjoys reading, cooking, listening to music and traveling.

Website: kimberlyjbenoit.com
Newsletter: kimberlyjbenoit.com/newsletter/
LinkedIn: www.linkedin.com/in/kimberly-j-benoit/

9
KRYSTAL CHAMPLIN-GERAGE

THERE'S NO SECRET TO SUCCESS: TAKE ACTION AND RESULTS WILL FOLLOW

What does it take to become a successful entrepreneur? Does one start their dream business and wake up successful one morning with a plethora of clients who are the perfect fit? Is there a secret answer to guarantee success?

The truth is that there is no secret answer that guarantees success for entrepreneurs. There is no one decision, one action, or one "thing" that an entrepreneur can do that ensures sheer perfection and the "happily ever after" in business.

In fact, there are some key statistics regarding entrepreneurship that should be kept in mind. While the following stats may be uncomfortable to read, the purpose is to show that there is no magic in creating and maintaining a successful business over time. It is a process that requires ongoing work.

According to the US Bureau of Labor Statistics...

- One in five businesses fail within the first year, and it does not matter whether it's run by an entrepreneur or if it's a larger business. This works out to 18.4% of businesses,
- Of the businesses that make it in that first year, 30% do not make it past the second year,
- About 38% of the remaining businesses close their doors by the third year.

And the percentage of the businesses that close keeps increasing. At the 10-year mark, 65% have shut their doors. Of course, there can be numerous reasons, including financial matters impacting the businesses. The statistics above reflect the timeline between March 2011 and March 2021. So, of course, we must remember that many of the businesses that shut down at the ten-year mark may have likely been severely impacted by the pandemic, especially since we do not have a breakdown by industry or knowledge of why they failed.

When I first started out with my first consulting business, I faced several obstacles which I eventually overcame. The idea of overcoming adversity, being disciplined, and fearless was unknown to me. So, you may ask why I became an entrepreneur and own several businesses. The answer is because I always had an internal pull to do something more and impact others in this world. I knew the risks going in, and I still hold them dear today. The way I overcome these challenges was reading as many books on starting a business, reaching out to mentors in my field, reaching out to strangers who I found to be successful, got a few certifications that would help me create a framework for my clients, and simply believing this is the path I was meant to take. Today, I run two businesses, one is a consulting company for law firm management because let's face it, attorneys go to law school to practice law not run a law firm like a true business. My other is a coaching company where we work with emerging leaders to become catalysts for change within their organizations. Here are some things I learnt on my journey.

WHAT CAUSES ENTREPRENEURS TO FAIL?

A pandemic isn't the only circumstance that causes a business to sink or that causes entrepreneurs to throw in the towel. Understanding the main causes of failure in advance is crucial. It helps active entrepreneurs and those with an entrepreneurial spirit mitigate the causes.

There's no clear vision for the business. While there's always room for change and improvement, entrepreneurs shouldn't start a "business" without anything in mind. The purpose of the vision is to help the entrepreneur determine where they want their business to be in the future. Even a one-sentence starter is better than nothing. If there is at least one sentence, there is something to begin working from, something to consider, something to add onto as the entrepreneur begins to expand their thoughts. As the saying goes, "Where there is no vision, the people perish." Start working on putting the vision into writing.

The niche isn't properly defined. While the term "niche" seems to have become a buzzword, what it really means is "specialization" or "target audience for the business." An entrepreneur must be able to define their specialization or who their business serves. Not all businesses are designed to act as generalists. Of course, some can act as a generalist, but it's also crucial to segment the general audience and understand their buying habits to create the proper marketing campaigns. Yet, many creative entrepreneurs and even tech entrepreneurs (or technopreneurs) must provide that specialization. The old saying, "You can't be everything to everyone" rings true even in business. It's better to show yourself as the expert in one or two industries as your business begins and include related industries as you grow. Choose industries you know and understand, especially if they will most benefit from what your business provides.

There is no business plan. A business plan is vital for entrepreneurs for several reasons. The importance of having and keeping the business plan updated will vary depending on the immediate and future goals of the entrepreneur. As a whole, a business plan holds all of an entrepreneur's other plans. It's a roadmap of how an entrepreneur plans to run the business. It's important to recognize that a business plan is not set in stone. Entrepreneurship is fluid. As the business changes, the business plan can also change. The plan includes information about how marketing will take place, which services will be offered and to which industries they will be offered, and how ROI will be determined for marketing methods, growth metrics, and financials. The financials are important for the entrepreneur to measure growth and for entrepreneurs who may wish to seek out financial backing of some kind.

The entrepreneur takes no action. Many say, "I'm an entrepreneur," when asked what they do. However, they have nothing to show for it. If there's no action taken to start, build, run, and grow the business, it never starts; it falls apart, becomes stagnant, and fails. There is no perfect moment to launch. There is no perfect moment to work on toward success. The six-hour binge of a series that's being streamed or mindlessly scrolling and not really absorbing what's in front of your eyes is tIme that could be devoted to business growth.

There is a lack of consistency. Think of the industry you want to serve. Who is your dream client in that industry? Think of a successful entrepreneur that you admire because they are, to you, the pinnacle of success. Consider how each made it to where they are now. It wasn't from inconsistency. Entrepreneurs who want to be successful in their field and with their target market must be consistent. It is a daily commitment.

There is no interest in learning. Although entrepreneurs are creative and often innovative leaders who carve their own paths, there are times when learning is a must. This could be local courses, books, continuing education, various online courses, etc. Technology touches every industry and every business. Marketing models change. It's imperative for success that entrepreneurs are interested in learning.

If you can mitigate the likelihood of facing the most common failures experienced by entrepreneurs, then you might be able to prevent them from happening. You now possess the ability to plan for them in advance. Can entrepreneurs use any learned skills to give them a better opportunity to succeed? The answer is yes, provided that the entrepreneur **takes action** to leverage the power of the skills.

STRIVING FOR SUCCESS: CAN YOU STACK THE DECK?

There are several skills that can help entrepreneurs **become and remain** successful. These skills can be learned by any entrepreneur. They can help you feel more confident, control your time, get more completed during the time devoted to work, understand your target market and other people better, and how to set goals that you can achieve.

Emotional Intelligence as an Entrepreneur

Emotional intelligence is knowing how to discern, control, and assess emotions. Why is this a pertinent skill for success? Isn't business... business? Yes, it's business. However, entrepreneurs with an immense understanding of emotional intelligence generally...

- Possess more empathy for others,
- Become better problem solvers,
- Possess better social skills,
- Form strong, beneficial relationships.

Emotional intelligence gives an entrepreneur the ability to manage their own emotions. It also allows entrepreneurs to recognize, honor, and assist in managing the emotions of those around them. In short, it helps an entrepreneur become "a people person."

People as a whole want to do business with people they like and trust. When we consider the people we like and trust, one of the things we most likely name about why we like and trust them is that they *know* us: our moods, our feelings, and who we are.

It's clear how this can be helpful with colleagues, prospects, and employees. It's also a beneficial tool to use in your marketing. As you get to know individuals who belong to your target market, you're able to better design marketing campaigns that speak directly to them. This may include creating buyer personas that address specific traits found within their personalities, where the decision-makers are in their career (such as upper management), and how what your business offers directly impacts their pain points.

There are multiple online courses, books, websites, and online articles designed to teach people how to develop and improve their emotional intelligence.

DEVELOP AND DISPLAY EXECUTIVE PRESENCE

Do you *feel* like an executive? As the person who started the business, you *are* its Chief Executive Officer. If you're the only person involved in starting the business, you're also the Chief Financial Officer, the Marketing Director, and HR Director. Perhaps you're also the Bookkeeper. When starting out, entrepreneurs act in every role necessary to keep the business running.

Do you *feel* like an executive, or do you *feel* like an imposter? At some point in starting and running a business, and usually, at many points, every entrepreneur faces imposter syndrome. Yet, even without discussing imposter syndrome, many entrepreneurs do not feel as if they are executives.

How can you develop and display an executive presence? First, we must define executive presence. An executive presence is a person's ability to act in a way that is decisive and dignified while they embody the classic elements of leadership. Someone with an executive presence has leadership skills that show through. For example, you may see that they...

- Work well under pressure; they do not snap at others,
- Clearly communicate with others regardless of whether they are communicating with clients, vendors, or employees,
- Present a confident and calm persona; they choose to be proactive instead of reactive in situations.

After reading that definition, who comes to your mind? That person has an executive presence. Maybe it is naturally part of who they are, but it is just as likely that they had to learn or refine some of the skills involved.

How does one manage to build an executive presence? It is, after all, an essential skill that can contribute to the success of any entrepreneur. Here are some tips:

- Practice keeping your feelings under control when you are involved in high-stress situations. Executive presence means staying calm when you're under pressure and avoiding emotional outbursts.
- Practice your communication skills. Learn to communicate efficiently and clearly. Learn to control your tone of voice.
- Master active listening. The ability to listen to your clients, potential clients, and your employees cannot be understated.

- Share your goals for the future. This helps raise morale and increase motivation, especially if you're enthusiastic.
- Understand how others see you and interact with you. This is not an exercise of "This is who I am; take it or leave it." As you look to grow your business, it becomes important to receive more referrals or network with more people who may need what your business offers. People need to trust you and have confidence in you as someone who can meet their needs. You must **be** that person. Talk with people in your circle about how you are perceived in different types of situations, including high-stress situations. This will give you insight into who you currently are. You will know what you need to improve on to improve yourself and, therefore, your business in the future.

FEELING AND LOOKING YOUR BEST

Society has entered a period where remote work and virtual businesses are the norm. It's just as accepted to run a business out of your home as it is to lease a brick-and-mortar space. For the purposes of marketing in certain industries that do not require licensing to provide services or goods, geography is essentially dead.

We've entered the "PJ Era," where it's become acceptable to spend every day working in one's pajamas or sweats. While there are certain occasions where this may be sufficient attire, is it really good for entrepreneurs to do it every day?

At some point, entrepreneurs can face burnout while working in their pajamas, from their couch, while binge-watching the latest fad show. And their creativity, the love of what they do, their clients, and their profit will pay the price.

For entrepreneurs just starting out to those who work from home to those who routinely meet in person or online with potential and current clients, should they get dressed and look their best to feel their best? Is there science behind that concept?

Yes, there is some science behind this concept. When we begin the process of looking our best, it stimulates our brain to subconsciously remember a time when we felt great. Perhaps we were more productive. Perhaps something successful happened that day. The cues help us feel empowered and positive.

FINDING YOUR TRIBE AS AN ENTREPRENEUR

Entrepreneurs need a community. Being part of a community can provide your business with more opportunities. It provides more colleagues (and friends as you get to know them) to talk with about business and life. It's vital to build or join a community that includes people with the same interests and vision as you.

What does it take to build a community or to find your tribe?

- If you're building a community online or looking online, one of the easiest ways is to choose a social media platform, such as Twitter, and begin searching for hashtags that match what you do. For example, there's a #marketingtwitter and a #lawtwitter. Get involved in conversations. With some time, you can determine who is part of your tribe. You can use Zoom to host conversations for deeper discussions.
- If you're looking offline, contact the Chamber of Commerce in your area to find out if there are networking events, conferences, and workshops available for you to attend. Libraries are another excellent opportunity since they also have events. These are opportunities for you to get to know people in your area that may become part of your tribe after you get to know them.
- Let your friends and colleagues know you're looking to network with others who share your vision and motivation.

They may be able to introduce you to others. The key here is in the specificity of what you are telling your friends and colleagues. You are not looking to network with just anyone; you're looking to network with **others who share your vision and motivation.**

- Stay in touch with your tribe. Do not allow yourself to fall into the mindset of "If they would contact me, I would respond." Take it upon yourself to send the email, direct message, or text. You become the accountability partner.
- Keep it interesting. It can be easy to fall away from the group if no one looks forward to attending. Your tribe should create a plan that includes things you can do together, even if it is online, so that all of you continue to look forward to attending.

WHAT ABOUT MENTORS?

How does an entrepreneur go about choosing the right mentor? Mentorship is often a misunderstood concept. Of course, there is the unofficial mentor that you admire. Perhaps they know and are gracious enough to answer the occasional question. However, an official mentorship is considerably different. It starts with you locating someone you not only admire but someone who **shares the same values as you in business.** It's also good if they are in the same industry, but it's not a requirement.

Mentorship requires an investment of time from the mentor and the mentee. Because of this, it's imperative that you ask this person whether they have the time and desire to be your mentor. You should also ask how many times per month (one or two) they can devote to speaking with you. How long can they talk with you during those times? Will this be over the phone or through Zoom?

Because your new mentor is going out of their way, it is crucial that you are respectful of their time. Come to each meeting prepared with questions or topics. Listen, take notes, and ask questions. Make an action plan. Talk about your results and the failures you experienced between calls. It is not the job of your mentor to keep you accountable. Their job is to guide you with experience. It is your responsibility to be accountable to them.

EFFICIENT TIME MANAGEMENT: TIME BLOCKING

Entrepreneurs need to have critical time management skills. Until the 1990s, multitasking was considered the perfect model for time management. Yet, it was eventually shown that working on multiple tasks at one time not only took longer to finish the tasks but also increased the likelihood of errors.

In 2016, Cal Newport's Deep Work took the entrepreneurial world by storm. The premise is that blocking off 60 to 90 minutes at a time for undistracted work on one project can improve your professional abilities and help you complete more work.

There are multiple websites, videos, and planners devoted to both Deep Work and time blocking, also referred to as time boxing. The underlying premise of time blocking is this:

- Prioritize your task list in advance. This helps ensure that your focus isn't constantly distracted by last-minute decisions.
- Choose an amount of time for tasks and place them on your calendar.
- Work on that task on that day for the specified amount of time. Perhaps you block out four hours on one day to work on several things for one client. Then, after a break, you block off two hours to work on something for another client.
- Do you see blank spots? Great. You can leave those alone. They provide you with room to move things around when life happens.

Time blocking assists in eliminating perfectionism and teaches you how to say no because you have a real-life view of your calendar.

90-DAY GOALS V. WEEKLY GOALS: WHICH SHOULD YOU USE?

Four quarters make up a year. Entrepreneurs know what they want to make in a year. Even when starting out, they usually know what goals they want to meet in their first year. If an entrepreneur takes their yearly financial goal and divides it by four, they see what needs to be met before expenses every 90 days. Here's an example to keep the math simple:

An entrepreneur's goal is $100,000 in their first year. When this figure is divided by four, it becomes $25,000. The 90-day financial goal becomes $25,000. This may not be the only meaningful goal for the business. However, 90 days is certainly enough time to accomplish one-fourth of the yearly goal. We will come back to this number in a moment.

However, it's crucial that 90-day goals (and annual goals) are reasonable. To set 90-day goals, consider possible goals and write them down. Choose three to five quarterly goals. Write them out clearly so that they can be measured. Again, though, make sure they are reasonable. They should be something that can be accomplished in 90 days.

Create a plan that gets you to your goals. This includes creating weekly goals. For example, what sort of weekly monetary goal would you need to fulfill if the quarterly goal is $25,000? There are 12 weeks in 90 days. We take $25,000 and divide it by 12. Weekly, the business would need to bring in $2, 083.33. From there, you could determine the number of goods or services that would need to be sold and how to make that happen.

All goals can also be modified. If your goals appear too difficult to reach or too easy, they can be modified. Sometimes proper goal-setting for entrepreneurs takes practice.

REFLECTING AND IMPLEMENTING A PLAN

As you reflect on the advice I shared here, I hope there is something that sparks your interest to help you on your entrepreneurial journey. Over the course of my career, the one piece of advice that I share over and over is to reflect on your vision, write it down, and take action. It doesn't matter what action that is but over time it compounds and results start to show. So, I encourage you to get out your journal, start to write what your vision looks like, and pick an action to take tomorrow. It doesn't matter what it is. Just get started.

ABOUT THE AUTHOR

KRYSTAL CHAMPLIN-GERAGE

Krystal Champlin-Gerage is a consultant and business advisor with RJH Consulting and Maverick Coaching Solutions. In her roles, she brings over a decade of experience and expertise to law firms and small businesses across the nation. When working with clients, she empowers them to develop a growth mindset that enables them to take control of their careers and organizations. Her methodology leads clients to build profitable and sustainable businesses based on their core values and definition of success.

Ms. Champlin-Gerage holds several certifications that she applies to her client work. She is a Certified Executive Coach, Certified Emotional Intelligence Practitioner, Certified DiSC Trainer, and holds a Six Sigma Lean certification.

She enjoys working with professionals at every level on learning the "business side" of their organizations. She has used her experience and knowledge to help her clients envision the next level of growth while providing the accountability, support, and guidance they need during the process. She enjoys the challenge of helping her clients distinguish between contentment versus complacency and become a catalyst for change in their industries.

Website: www.rjhconsulting.com

www.maverickcoachingsolutions.com
LinkedIn: www.linkedin.com/in/krystalchamplin
Email: krystal@maverickcoachingsolutions.com

10
MEGAN DOUGHERTY

THE SECRET TO SUCCESSFUL PODCASTING FOR YOUR BUSINESS

In 2017, I was what you might call burnt out. Having left a fast-paced and fast-growing internet marketing startup the year prior, I was at professional loose ends, dead-tired from hustle culture and the industry I was working in.

The whole internet marketing environment—or the ways and means by which people were building their businesses selling information and services digitally—was exhausting me. It all felt so bad. Many of the standard best practices felt exploitative and misleading. And there was no one culprit, no first source you could point at and say: "There. That's what's wrong with internet marketing."

It's pervasive throughout the industry, and all justified in the most glowing of language. "We're just looking at the data and making decisions accordingly," to explain manipulative language in webinars. "People need to be responsible for their buying choices," while writing a sales page that pushes the bounds of truth to an alarming degree. "It will work if they do the work correctly," while wording a guarantee such that any minuscule deviation or modification to fit a situation invalidates it. "It's a win-win," while compelling participants to provide free advertising for projects. "It's about privacy," while refusing to provide references or success metrics.

"It's the way it's done," while assigning too much work, gatekeeping content, selling aggressively, saying it can work for everyone, or otherwise, in all of the millions of possible ways, being a jerk.

And it's not any one individual's or company's fault. Most people learned what they're doing from trusted professionals in the space, who were themselves only doing what everyone else does because... it converts.

It's not everyone, of course, and it's not always. There are lots of lovely people with fabulous businesses being amazing citizens of the world and genuinely helping their clients and communities. But it was enough that I was sick of it and after 6 years, had a hair-trigger explosive response to anything even remotely tarred with the brush of internet marketing. Unfortunately, because internet marketing was the only thing I'd done for years and I no longer had the stomach for it, I was largely unemployable.

So, I puttered around, taking on a few freelance projects and running a few virtual events, which really was refreshing, until one day, an old colleague with a background in broadcast radio and a reputation for ironclad ethics reached out and said, "Hey, do you want to start a business?"

I said, "With you? Absolutely."

That colleague was Audra Casino, and we married her audio experience to my years in digital marketing, added some unbreakable rules about service standards and how we would treat people, and One Stone Creative was born.

We produce podcasts for businesses.

We chose to do this because there is a real, solid (as solid as digital files can be, anyway!) deliverable we can provide and services we can track, measure, and deliver (always on time, thank you very much.) We create something real and valuable for people, that we can describe clearly and honestly.

We're not out to change the world, and we're not out to get fabulously wealthy. We don't create expectations we can't fulfill; or work with people we don't think will benefit from it. There are six of us on the team, and we try to make the company a pleasant, engaging place to work with a strong focus on balance and exceptionally good service to our clients. Our guiding principle is simple: we do what we say we're going to do.

We help create podcasts that are valuable to the businesses making them. No muss, no fuss, no nonsense. And no pretending that a podcast is going to be a great fit for absolutely every business. It feels really good.

You can put down this book, open Google, type in "how to start a podcast" and find dozens of companies that will give you clear and accurate information about how to do it. But they can't tell you if that choice will be ideal for your business. There is, happily, one 'secret' that will help you determine, today, if it might be.

It's a step that is overlooked surprisingly often when people and companies start new shows. Most people start looking at the tech and the platforms and trying to get guests or get over their nerves about recording—that is all important! But it doesn't really impact whether your podcast will be successful.

The secret to successful podcasting for business *is having a business purpose for your podcast* and associated metrics that you can track to see whether it's actually working for you. It's not sexy (unless you're as into spreadsheets as I am), but it's effective. Our clients podcast for years when the average show on the internet tends to last under two months.

This is because we start them with a real, solid business reason for existing, and we track progress towards the success of that goal. And if we stop making progress, we address it openly and decide if it makes sense to continue. Sometimes it does, and sometimes it doesn't.

It amazes me how often this is left out of the discussion about podcasting as a business.

I was giving a talk on podcasting to a group of financial services marketers a few years ago—and these are professionals at the top of their game. I asked the room: "Who here has a podcast?" About half of the people in that room raised their hands. Then I asked: "Who here set a business goal for their podcast?" No one had.

So the first call I have with anyone who has been sent our way or found our business isn't really a sales call (although sometimes it results in a sale); it's an exploration and explanation of what podcasting can do for their business and if the results are what the business actually needs. It's also a chance to see if we sort of like each other enough to take a stab at working together.

And I've got it all here for you in this very chapter, so YOU can think about whether podcasting will really be a fit for your business. If it is, you can take it and run if you want to go in-house or use it to inform the conversations you have with third-party service providers you might speak with.

Let's go.

The first and most important thing you need to do is get clear on your business and/or marketing goals. The trick to making sure that a podcast is a good investment of your time, money and energy is looking at what podcasts CAN do and comparing that to what your business needs.

Let me say it again: before starting a podcast, you have to get clear on your business or marketing goals.

Stop reading right now and think about what your top three goals for the next six months are. You don't have to be too specific, and they don't need to be SMART. Think: more traffic, lower costs, better retention, more sales calls, more backlinks, that kind of thing. (Don't worry, serious and measurable metrics do come into play, just after you've decided whether a podcast is a good idea!)

Write them down before moving on.

1.

2.

3.

Got them down? Good. Now let's look at what podcasts can accomplish and see if anything matches up.

At a high level, there are three (and a half) main types of business podcasts, which we call the Business Podcast Blueprints, and if you're seriously considering starting a show, figuring out which Blueprint is going to be the best for your business is going to help you make all of the strategic decisions about it that you need to.

Within each Blueprint are various sub-goals that you can achieve. They can really be mixed and matched – you can optimize your podcast for anything you want to.

It breaks down like this:

High-Level Blueprint = Strategic decisions and role of the podcast in your business.

Individual Metrics = Determining if podcasting is a good fit for you and measuring success.

RELATIONSHIP BUILDING PODCASTS

Podcasts are a natural networking and conversation machine, and this type f podcast always has guests. If building out your professional connections is a top priority, this is the type of show to create. At each stage in your podcasting process, from booking a guest to promoting the episode, you have the opportunity to build relationships with people who could help your business.

For example,

- Lead generation,
- Networking,
- Partnership and JV relationships,
- Influencer marketing
- Affiliate arrangements etc.

AUDIENCE ENGAGEMENT PODCASTS

Audience Engagement Podcasts are all about connecting with an audience you already have that needs content from you for one reason or another. These might be fans of your books, speaking engagements you want to connect with at scale, or new leads coming into your pipeline who would benefit from a crash course in your topic area. You can be really creative with this kind of show.

Specific metrics you can track with this kind of podcast are the following:

- Social media engagement,
- Feedback on ideas,
- Top of funnel conversions,
- Internal training and culture building,
- Product and service sales.

THOUGHT LEADERSHIP PODCASTS

If you are trying to become more well-known in your industry as a serious thinker, innovator and authority, then this is the type of podcast you should have. The key thing to remember is that you need to be introducing your own IP in order to be a thought leader! You might want a mix of conversations with colleagues and connections and solo episodes.

These are some of the specific things a thought leadership podcast can help you achieve:

- Media mentions,
- Backlinks and citations,
- Invitations to collaborate and contribute,
- Speaking and Presenting opportunities,
- Shorter sales cycles.

And a half:

CONTENT PODCASTS

Creating a lot of content is just what happens when you podcast. That's why this is the "half" – you'll get it no matter what other priority you have, but it is also perfectly legitimate to podcast to get content out there and get content out there alone! Every week, or every other week, you're releasing an episode. That adds up to a lot of content over time.

Here are some ways you can measure the impact of that content on your business:

- Website traffic,
- SEO rankings,
- Guest post content,

- Social media content,
- Sales materials,
- Large Projects (like books and courses).

Remember, the blueprint is the high-level purpose of the show and the role it plays in your business—Relationship Building, Audience Engagement, Thought Leadership or Content. You can measure the success of the podcast FOR your business with any of the metrics suggested (or any others you can think of as long as you can track them!)

So, here's the critical question:

Are the goals you wrote down listed under one or more of the podcast types?

If yes, then amazing; a podcast could be a valuable part of your marketing strategy!

If no, then a podcast probably isn't a great investment for you right now, and you should prioritize other business and marketing activities. Open this up again in six months and see where you are. 😊

Assuming that a podcast could be useful for you, let's look at what having one would mean for your day-to-day working life—because while it's a high-value and efficient marketing activity, it's not an easy or low-effort one, nor is it inexpensive if you're doing it right.

I am going to list out some things you need to have in place or be prepared to add to your workflow to plan, create and promote a high-quality podcast.

- You need to like talking to people and people talking back across multiple platforms.
- You need to be comfortable with different technology platforms like Apple Podcasts, your website backend, a

podcast host, social media accounts and an audio-recording interface or have access to a team or freelancers that are.
- You need to have about 2 hours of prep and recording time for every 45 minutes of finished audio. (This can be lessened slightly if you have a great assistant!)
- You need to have a good quality mic and a reasonably quiet recording location.
- You need to have about 3-5 hours of time to edit every 45 minutes of finished audio or an editor who can do it for you. This time investment varies depending on the type of editing you need to do, but that's a subject for another time. (If you are doing it yourself or in-house, it will start off taking forever, but you'll get faster, don't worry!)
- You need to have at least an hour for each episode to promote it—and more if possible!
- You need to be able to set specific goals for your content and have a mechanism in place to make sure you're meeting them.

Those are the really critical elements you need to have. And as you can tell, getting help makes things a lot easier. That help can be an enthusiastic team member who is excited to learn the ropes, a freelance podcast editor—of whom there are many—or an agency ready to take care of pretty much everything except the part where you talk.

Those are the things you absolutely need to have to create a podcast, but there are a few more technically optional ones that can make a huge difference in terms of how pleasant the workflow is for you and how successful your show ultimately is.

If possible, you should do the following:

- Have time dedicated after each episode to repurpose a few elements from it.

- Have someone listen to your episodes and give you feedback on how to improve.
- Pitch yourself as a guest on other episodes to grow your podcast audience more quickly.
- Listen to other shows to note what you like, what you don't and what you want to start doing on your own.
- Create sharing materials to give your guests and fans to help them spread the word.
- Occasionally email your community to let them know of particularly interesting episodes.

If you read all of these and found yourself nodding your head and saying, "Yeah, I could do that, or get that. This could be great!" Then you, my friend, should start a podcast.

If you read all this and found yourself thinking "there is no way a podcast is worth all of that." Then podcasting will probably make you miserable, and you should explore other avenues instead.

At the end of the day, creating an effective business podcast comes down to what you actually *need* to achieve your goals—a show can be pretty bare bones and still meet its objectives. Depending on the goals you're working towards, you may want to invest more or fewer resources. And depending on your budget, available time and tolerance for admin, you may want to do it in-house or hire a third-party service provider.

A podcast will not be an easy project, and it will not gain traction immediately. It takes time, practice, and a willingness to look at and be led by the data. But when it's working for you, it can be a powerful flywheel of content and relationships that helps your business thrive.

And that is an amazing thing to have.

ABOUT THE AUTHOR

MEGAN DOUGHERTY

Megan Dougherty is a digital business strategist and the Co-Founder of One Stone Creative, a podcast production agency that focuses on creating high-value podcasts for companies and business owners. Every business is unique, and so is the role a podcast can play in it. Using the Business Podcast Blueprints framework, One Stone Creative helps business owners, thought leaders and marketing managers develop and distribute podcasts that hit key business objectives – in a surprising variety of ways! Megan hosts the Business Podcast Blueprint Show, and publishes the annual State of Business Podcasting Report. She lives in Western Quebec with her spouse and dozens of thriving houseplants.

Free email series on how to Optimize, Automate and Grow a Company Podcast - for planned or existing shows!
OneStoneCreative.net/OAG
One Stone Creative: OneStoneCreative.net
Twitter: twitter.com/OneStoneC

11

YURY LEVCHENKOV

EVERYTHING IS POSSIBLE

I'm the kind of person who likes to make a point, so I'll share with you the business formulas—the ones that you can easily apply here and now. These basic formulas have emerged from many experiences, including trials, successes and failures. They are refined and effective and can be used in small businesses.

According to my survey, most people who make their first significant money before the age of 18 develop into entrepreneurs.

I had already established my first business, a beauty salon, at the beginning of 2000. At the time, I had no idea that this was probably one of the most complicated business ventures. I remember well when, after a lot of hard work, long nights and searches, the business started to bring its first profit. However, the thought that I really had no idea what I was doing never left. I asked myself many questions, wondering if I was running my business correctly, but I came up with more questions than answers.

I interviewed hundreds of my clients who were running various small and large businesses. I asked which business management strategy brought them the most profit, customer traffic, and recognition. To my surprise, 90% of respondents said they achieved their results "somehow".

So, I am also an example of "somehow". Only in the long run did I realise that the result was exactly the same—"something".

After smoothly running my business for 20 years with the "somehow" strategy, my business finally began to seriously falter. I then began to explore other methods of running a business. These are simple, and they work. They produce mindblowing results and have changed the lives of many entrepreneurs. However, I want to emphasise the importance of changing your thinking and actions in order to achieve sustainable business success.

5NEW

The 5NEW (five new jobs per day) method has been the most effective for me. Once you understand it, it usually eliminates the need for other methods.

An entrepreneur with 50 employees was constantly stuck in a cycle of routine work— morning to evening—and all responsibility rested on his shoulders. When I told him about the 5NEW method, he came back after a week of implementing it and told me his employees could now work independently and take the initiative.

The following week, I heard: "Oh, everything is so great that it's almost scary. I no longer have routine jobs. What should I do now? Everyone around is running around, buzzing, working. I don't know what they're doing, but I'm seeing amazing results."

And as the month ended, I heard the phrase that surprised me the most: "I want another business. I want to expand!"

The 5NEW method does not only work immediately; the results are permanent. It empowers employees to take charge and aim for improved output without your intervention or control.

In most small businesses, the biggest obstacle to breakthrough is often the management. So how does it work?

- The manager comes up with a new idea - he becomes an obstacle because he came up with work for others. Therefore, he remains guilty.
- The manager tells you to work and bring results. Guilty again.
- The manager needs reasoned decisions; otherwise, you will not get approval. Guilty.
- The manager needs a report, and the employee has a bunch of excuses if he doesn't have one yet. Guilty again.

These are just a few examples of how the leader is usually to blame. It seems to result from an ancient and utterly dysfunctional business model dating back to the 80s. With 5NEW, everything is different.

INSTALLATION

It's important to remember that the 5NEW method is delivered one-to-one. That's the only way you'll see results. You will need an hour and a half per worker that needs a breakthrough. Sit down with the worker in a tranquil environment and talk about the company's philosophy, objectives, and vision. Talk about your personal viewpoint, dreams, and what objectives are important to you and why they are essential to the company.

After about an hour of your personal monologue, entrust the employee with a single job or mission. It could sound like this: "Since you understand what and why this is important, starting tomorrow, you'll have to do five new tasks that lead the company towards progress." You can start with two to three jobs a day, but the goal is five in the long run.

These are not routine, everyday tasks such as checking emails but something that has not yet been tried. The employee has to come up with those themselves.

So what happened here? You just passed the ball of responsibility into the hands of the employee. The employee becomes responsible for their working day, and the manager ceases to be an obstacle since work is carried out according to the employee's wishes.

CONTROL

As a manager, you may wonder how to ensure that the employee performs those tasks effectively. However, the employee is in control, not you. You can request the employee to perform a personal audit or report. This may sound like this: "Please write down what you did last week/yesterday. Write down those five completed jobs, and then please present it orally and in writing."

Such a request will make the employee stop and understand that they really have to work. However, it will take time for this system to establish itself. It is not uncommon for an employee's first reaction to be negative, but after a while, they accept it and take action. But if the employee can't provide a list of completed tasks, activities, and results, the question becomes about what they're doing in your company after all.

LEADER

The leader (head of the company) is someone whose energy must be directed to two main points:

- Vision - where are we going? Direction and purpose - which way are we going?
- Resource. Takes care of resources for the implementation of goals.

The rest, mostly routine tasks, don't have to be on the leader's shoulder; they must be distributed to the team. Otherwise, when the routine falls on the leader's shoulders, there is no time and energy left for strategic work, which is a key component of a successful business.

• • •

BALL OF RESPONSIBILITY GAME

The Responsibility Ball Game is a psychological game that digs into who is responsible and to whom. How does it work?

According to my surveys, 90% of the issue in most small businesses is the employees. This is usually due to their unwillingness to work, inability to collaborate, and failure to understand how to achieve a result. And then, the manager has a big task of communicating with the employees in a way that both sides understand everything.

Passing the ball of responsibility is a common problem in most small businesses.

The responsibility ball game is a psychological act when people do not take responsibility but pass it on to someone else.

Here's an example:

The employee comes to the manager with the message of an offer for the business. The ball of responsibility is dropped on the manager.

Manager: "Please read the proposal by lunchtime, scrutinise it, and present our three possible choices. I will wait for a 3-minute presentation with thoughts and arguments at 2 p.m." The ball of responsibility is again in the hands of the employee.

Another common case occurs when customers approach a business without specific wishes but with high expectations. An often-heard phrase goes like this: "Do whatever you want. I trust you."

While the business may appreciate the vote of confidence, this too is passing the ball of responsibility. And if the business receives that ball thinking that they will definitely do their best, it creates the basis for a conflict since their best may not be what the customer expects.

So the phrase "do whatever you want; I trust you" usually translates to "take the responsibility of making the decision for me, and if I don't like it, then you're screwed..."

I've witnessed this phrase so many times throughout my career, and the common cause is always the shifting of responsibility.

So listen to employee-customer interactions, and you will quickly recognise the pattern of how this "game" is played. Even in relationships, it is common to pass around the blame ... "you are to blame because I didn't expect that," or "that's not what I meant."

The responsibility ball can be destructive when one person shoulders too many responsibilities. I've seen plenty of entrepreneurs in business with bags full of balls of responsibility. They are tired and stuck in a routine—I used to be like that too. Let's share responsibilities as equally as possible. So, seek out the initiator of the game in your business and adjust rules to govern the distribution of responsibility.

• • •

WORD

WORD is when employees are constantly talking—BLA, BLA, BLA, like ducks in a swamp—but nothing happens.

If someone asked me to give one piece of advice to a business newcomer, it would be to ban talking about non-work topics and enable EXCEL spreadsheets if the specifics of your job allow it. There is nothing better than having everything presented in black and white, neatly and consistently organised. EXCEL is a clear plan, and structured information. EXCEL doesn't only refer to numbers in finance; it means clarity and security.

WORD – what is it?

It is a Windows writing program, a place for your chaotic thoughts. It's like meeting an acquaintance who talks a lot and in the end you don't even understand what the conversation was about. WORD is chaos and uncertainty, but business is about numbers. In order to organise the chaos, you have to see it clearly. WORD is perfect for this.

WORD, in that general war (that's what I call team meetings) where everyone is shouting and screaming that something was always needed, something was missing so that the work would be done properly. However, no matter how many needs you satisfy, you need more and more. This is nothing but passing the ball of responsibility to the manager. Then the weekend would come, and everyone would go to rest, leaving the leader with a bag full of "balls" for the weekend. In my case, I used my weekends to complete my employees' tasks—I know many other leaders do the same. I accepted the whole bag myself, and it took me a while to understand how everything worked.

Now my meetings are short, specific, systematic and documented.

• • •

MEETINGS

MEETING PROCEDURE:

- At the beginning of the meeting, we look at the minutes of the previous meeting and the set goals. We clarify what we have done. Where are we stuck, and why? What resources are needed? What unexpected situations are we facing?
- During this discussion, tasks and goals for the next list automatically appear, and we record them again.
- We discuss what conclusions we make.

I used to hold meetings whose main goal was solving company issues. They were long, sometimes heated, and occasionally silent. Piles of advice came my way. After the meetings, I used to be in a hurry to apply the advice. I was burdened with additional work, other people's opinions and instructions on which way to turn here.

Discussions and empty advice without any clear plan of action is throwing the ball of responsibility away from yourself. During meetings, employees sometimes clearly tell you non-verbally to go away and that they will not take the ball.

And I, as a manager and a responsible person, work responsibly with the collected balls. Only there were a lot of those balls, and the work led me to close the business.

In my current business, we as a team know what responsibility is and try to distribute it evenly using the techniques described.

• • •

THREE GIGANTIC QUESTIONS

The manager needs to ask only three questions that help you not get involved in empty talk.

1. What did you do?

2. What do you plan to do next?

3. What resource is required for this?

3/7/90

This is my favourite philosophy.

- 90% are boat people for whom only two things are important:

1. Remuneration

2. Get paid ahead of time

With such employees, you will not swim long or far in a small business.

- 3% - these are people who want to change and are changing the world. They are always full of ideas and energy. They are constantly researching. You can't stop them. They are the ones doing the business.
- 7% - these are supportive people.

So my recommendation is, if you are a strong 3%, surround yourself with the 7%. Only people who support you. The right environment in business will allow you to reach great heights.

• • •

6-MONTH STRATEGIC SESSION

Big companies set annual goal plans. They are strictly followed and implemented. In small businesses, everything is a little different. We need a six-month preliminary plan so that we don't get off course as the months go by. External forces considered minor in large businesses affect small businesses significantly. Therefore, half a year for planning is a suitable period for any small business.

By mid-year, we need to review whether we're sailing in the right direction and how we are doing.

The 6-month STRATEGIC SESSION is when you gather with the 7% who support you, and for 59 minutes in a free form, you "put together" your investments and large-scale plans and refine the most important investments as the backbone of your goals for the next six months.

For example, the idea was born to participate in exhibitions where EnzoOrganic products successfully attract many new customers every year without leaving them indifferent. Of course, directions change and diversify depending on what is useful for the client, but it is important to record all, even small, victories. Remember where you were half a year ago, but have big ambitions for the next six months.

• • •

1 MONTH'S PRODUCT FORUM

Once a month, meet with several key people and refine the first new idea, product, or project that would help the company progress towards the result. This is a new tool that ensures the company flourishes when implemented.

Even after writing this chapter, we continued to solve many challenges as a business. We have systematised the scripts that tell us what the customer says and what needs to be answered in order to make sales. We have introduced a new product that has been well received by our customers. We have concentrated on colouristic (mixing colours) and have even developed our own formulas. These are just a few of our many changes and innovations.

We also recently thought of buying a wooden bicycle. So that the company stands out for its originality. However, we soon got down to visualisations. We discussed how to do it. We engraved the Enzo-Organic logo on the bike. I am the founder of this cosmetic line; it is important to me. The tree and the message spread by the products I create fit perfectly together. The key words of Enzo's production are sustainability, naturalness, love for the world, safety and a first-class touch on the skin. My bike represents all of these values, and I have ridden this bike all over Lithuania. I recorded videos as I cycled through the greenery of Lithuania, taking Enzo Shower Gel with me. In the future, we will exhibit the bike at exhibitions and showcases. EVERYTHING IS POSSIBLE.

• • •

LOVE LETTER 25

This is an email you send on the 25th of each month to your top sellers, in companies with 20+ employees. It's important to always send this letter. It's EXCEL, clarity, and knowing where you're going and what you want your employees to achieve in the next month. This letter might look like this:

"Hello,

The new month is approaching. Please write down what you plan to do (or what sales you plan to make) for the next month."

What budget is needed for this? You'll receive an answer on the 26th and correct it. Maybe weak goals? Maybe too big a budget?

On the 27th, you forward your corrections and approve the resolutions.

• • •

1000% CONCENTRATION

When my first business failed, I started another. You would think that I should have already known how everything worked, but it was apparent that everything I knew until then did not work. Therefore, I came to a point where I started all over again. And the new beginning finally brought me a successful business. Building new processes came with many sleepless nights. I was once asked, "What percentage were you focused on a specific goal?"

I said without hesitation, "1000%."

And this is what I realised at the time: the result comes when you give 1000% of your attention to what you want. Your full attention and love should be placed on the processes that realise your visions every day. Apply this method, and you will get results in no time. The fulfilment of your dream will come within reach, and small goals will lead to the fulfilment of one big one and program you for movement and energy for the future.

Give all your strength to the process. Stay focused on the goal. Each day, drop by drop, will bring big wins in the finale.

TIME FOR YOURSELF

This is a necessary aspect of a business. I know people who change the world. They work a lot and practically do not get out of the routine. They always have an endless list of tasks. They, like me, sometimes forget to rest. They push themselves to their extent and plan even more work. They usually don't even remember the last time they enjoyed themselves.

How do you learn the most difficult lesson of self-love? How do you learn to spare time for yourself? Simple: by force. At least in the beginning. Go to another city or to the park and just walk for 3 hours without a phone or access to the internet. Go to the spa, drink some tea, and let yourself be massaged with relaxing clay, honey, or anything that helps you relax. You may not want to but do it, and then do it two more times. Take a half-day nap in a relaxing bath or on the beach. Reserve a table at a luxury restaurant for yourself. And by no means spare the resource you give away—believe me, you get much more. Until you try and live in your skin, you will not fully understand the whole meaning.

ABOUT THE AUTHOR

YURY LEVCHENKOV

Yury is a successful entrepreneur in beauty and cosmetics retail industries. He grew his passion into reality by creating a cosmetics line, named after his son - Enzo-organic and made a 6-figure income within the first 2 years. He now empowers and inspires entrepreneurs to succeed in their businesses.

Yury's journey to success is based on mastering phenotype biology and consequently creating a simple strategic formula for business - 012, 5NEW.

Yury's journey to creating a successful business has not always been straight forward. He reveals he had to overcome "chaos" to get to where he is now. He says: "I had a lot of 'advisors' trying to tell me how I should be doing things, and too often I listened to them instead of listening to myself. Then I was hit with a period of apathy, and gradually my whole business, and my marriage, started to collapse.

LinkedIn: www.linkedin.com/in/yury-levchenkov-2540a51a7/
Instagram: www.instagram.com/enzo_organic/
Website: www.enzo-organic.com/

12

ABOUT THE PUBLISHER

DINA BEHRMAN

Inspired World Publishing was founded by former journalist Dina Behrman. It publishes solo and multi-author books from entrepreneurs, changemakers and business leaders with a story to tell and expertise to share.

As a publisher and PR strategist Dina works with entrepreneurs who want to inspire millions, skyrocket their visibility and attract more soulmate clients. She helps them stop being the internet's best kept secret, become the 'go to' expert and create a much bigger impact in the world by sharing their story and expertise in bestselling books and in the press.

She launched her business following a decade working as a journalist, during which she was published in virtually every national UK newspaper and many magazines. She's worked as a publicist for a number of 7-figure business owners, and has also helped hundreds of entrepreneurs learn how to do their own PR. She's been featured in Forbes, Entrepreneur, Huff Post, The Guardian, BBC radio, amongst others.

To find out more or to join her next multi-author book visit www.dinabehrman.com

Printed in Great Britain
by Amazon

10912575R00081